Harriet Beecher Stowe • Charles Edwar Lyman Beecher Stowe

Publisher's Note

The book descriptions we ask booksellers to display prominently warn that this is an historic book with numerous typos or missing text; it is not indexed or illustrated.

The book was created using optical character recognition software. The software is 99 percent accurate if the book is in good condition. However, we do understand that even one percent can be an annoying number of typos! And sometimes all or part of a page may be missing from our copy of the book. Or the paper may be so discolored from age that it is difficult to read. We apologize and gratefully acknowledge Google's assistance.

After we re-typeset and design a book, the page numbers change so the old index and table of contents no longer work. Therefore, we often remove them; otherwise, please ignore them.

Our books sell so few copies that you would have to pay hundreds of dollars to cover the cost of our proof reading and fixing the typos, missing text and index. Instead we let most customers download a free copy of the original typo-free scanned book. Simply enter the barcode number from the back cover of the paperback in the Free Book form at www.RareBooksClub.com. You may also qualify for a free trial membership in our book club to download up to four books for free. Simply enter the barcode number from the back cover onto the membership form on our home page. The book club entitles you to select from more than a million books at no additional charge. Simply enter the title or subject onto the search form to find the books.

If you have any questions, could you please be so kind as to consult our Frequently Asked Questions page at www. RareBooksClub.com/faqs.cfm? You are also welcome to contact us there.

General Books LLC™, Memphis, USA, 2012.

❧ ❧ ❧ ❧ ❧ ❧ ❧ ❧

HARRIET BEECHER STOWE THE STORY OF HER LIFE PREFACE

This life of Harriet Beecher Stowe is not a biography in the ordinary sense. It is rather the story of a real character; telling, not so much what she did as what she was, and how she became what she was.

Each of the ten chapters is meant to be complete in itself, and to tell how the child grew, how she became a teacher and writer, a wife and mother; and, as the author of " Uncle Tom's Cabin," rose from obscurity to fame. Then, we see her in the storm and stress of a war that she had done much to bring on; in her Southern home; as a delineator of New England life and character, and, finally, as she waits the muffled oar beside the silent sea and gently drifts away with the ebbing tide. She herself is ever at the centre, and everything else is subordinated to her and viewed through her consciousness, and we look at the facts of her life as they were mirrored there. What her critics in the past thought of her, or what they think of her in the present, or may think of her in the future, is not a matter that concerns us.

All that interests us is to know and to tell how the experiences of her life appeared to her, and how she appeared to herself. We are not so bold as to assume that our attempt has been entirely successful, but we are confident that the aim was well worth the effort.

We wish to express our obligation to Harper & Brothers for generously permitting us to utilize material contained in the "Autobiography and Correspondence of Lyman Beecher," and to Mrs. James T. Fields for her permission to use material to be found only in her invaluable "Life and Letters of Harriet Beecher Stowe."

Charles Edward Stowe.
Lyman Beecher Stowe.

New York, March 5, 1911.

CONTENTS

ILLUSTRATIONS

HARRIET BEECHER STOWE THE STORY OF HER LIFE CHAPTER I HOW THE CHILD GREW

Most of us have some recollections of early childhood which stand out in our minds as vividly as the most important events of later life. Harriet Beecher's earliest recollections were of her mother, who died September 25, 1816, when Harriet was five years old. She says of her mother, in describing the first of these incidents," Mother was an enthusiastic horticulturist in all small ways that her limited means allowed. Her brother John, in New York, had just sent her a small parcel of fine tulipbulbs. I remember rummaging these out of an obscure corner of the nursery one day when she was gone out, and being strongly seized with the idea that they were good to eat, and using all the little English I then possessed to persuade my brothers that these were onions such as grown people ate, and would be very nice for us. So we fell to and devoured the whole, and I recollect being somewhat disappointed at the odd sweetish taste, and thinking that onions were not as nice as I had supposed.

"Then mother's serene face appeared at the nursery door, and we all ran towards her and began to tell our discovery and achievement, — we had found this bag of onions and had eaten them all up!

"Also I remember that there was not even a momentary expression of impatience, but that she sat down and said, ' My dear children, what you have done makes mamma very sorry; those were not onions, but roots of beautiful flowers; and if you had let them alone, mamma would have had in the garden next summer great beautiful red and yellow flowers such as you never saw.' I remember how drooping and dispirited we all grew at this picture, and how sadly we regarded the empty paper bag."

This was one of the two incidents, which, as she says, "twinkle like rays through the darkness." The other was "of our all running and dancing out before her from the nursery to the sitting-groom one Sabbath morning, and her pleasant voice saying after us, 'Remember the Sabbath day to keep it holy.'"

She goes on to say, "Then I have a recollection of her reading to the children, one evening, Miss Edgeworth's 'Frank,' which had just come out, I believe, and was exciting a great deal of interest in the educational circles of Litchfield. After that I remember a time when every one said she was sick.... I

used to be permitted once a day to go into her room, where she lay bolstered up in bed. I have a vision of a very fair face with a bright red spot on each cheek, and a quiet smile as she offered me a spoonful of her gruel; of our dreaming one night, we little ones, that mamma had got well, and waking in loud transports of joy, and being hushed down by some one coming into the room. Our dream was indeed a true one. She was forever well; but they told us she was dead, and took us in to see something that seemed so cold and so unlike anything we had ever seen or known of her. "

Then came the funeral, which in those stern days had none of the soothing accessories of our gentler times. We are told of Harriet's little baby brother, Henry Ward, that after the funeral he was seen by his sister Catherine digging with great energy under her window, the bright sunlight shining through the long curls that hung down on either side of his little flushed face. When she asked what he was doing, he replied, " I 'm doing down to find mamma!"

"Although mother's bodily presence disappeared from our circle," says Mrs. Stowe, "I think that her memory and example had more influence in moulding her family, in deterring from evil and exciting to good, than the living presence of many mothers. It was a memory that met us everywhere, for every person in the town seemed to have been so impressed by her character and life that they constantly reflected some portion of it back upon us. The passage in 'Uncle Tom' where Augustine St. Clair describes his mother's influence is a simple reproduction of this mother's influence as it has always been in her family. " Such a woman was Roxana Foote, Doctor Lyman Beecher's first wife and the mother of eight of Doctor Beecher's eleven children.

The scenery of Litchfield, Connecticut, where Harriet Beecher was born June 14, 1811, had a deep and lasting effect upon the moulding of her character. Her lifelong love of nature was early cultivated by the rare beauty of Litchfield's hills and woods and streams. Of

these she says: —

"My earliest recollections of Litchfield are those of its beautiful scenery, which impressed and formed my mind long before I had words to give names to my emotions, or could analyze my mental processes. To the west of us rose a smoothbosomed hill, called Prospect Hill; and many a pensive, wondering hour have I sat at our playroom window, watching the glory of the wonderful sunsets that used to burn themselves out amid voluminous wreathings or castellated turrets of clouds proper to a mountainous region.

"On the east of us lay another upland, called Chestnut Hills, whose sides were wooded with a rich growth of forest trees, whose change of tint and verdure, from the first misty tints of spring green through the deepening hues of summer into the rainbow glories of autumn, was a subject of constant remark and expensive contemplation to us children. We heard them spoken of by older people and pointed out to visitors, and came to take pride in them as a sort of birthright. "

The house where Harriet was born was originally a square building with a hipped roof, to which before her birth her father had built an addition known as " the new part." In the " Autobiography and Correspondence of Lyman Beecher," it is described in part as follows: —

"The ground floor of the new part was occupied by a large parlor, in which memory recalls ministers' meetings with clouds of tobacco smoke, and musical soirees, with piano, flute, and song. Over this were sleeping-rooms, and in the attic was the study, the windows of which looked out into an apple orchard."

Mrs. Stowe wrote of this home and her father: "Father was very fond of music, and very susceptible to its influence; and one of the great eras of the family in my childish recollection is the triumphant bringing home from New Haven a finetoned upright piano, which a fortunate accident had brought within the range of a poor country minister's means. The ark of the covenant was not brought into the tabernacle with more gladness than this magical instrument into our abode. Father soon learned to accompany the piano on his violin in various psalm tunes and Scotch airs, and brothers Edward and William to perform their part on their flutes. So we had often domestic concerts which, if they did not attain to the height of artistic perfection, filled the house with gladness.

"One of the most decided impressions of the family, as it was in my childish days, was of a great household inspired by a spirit of cheerfulness and hilarity, and of my father, though pressed and driven with business, always lending an attentive ear to anything in the way of life and social fellowship. My oldest sister, whose life seemed to be a constant stream of mirthfulness, was his favorite and companion, and he was always more than indulgent towards her pranks and jokes. " This eldest sister says of her father, "I remember him more as a playmate than in any other character during my childhood." In spite of the fact that he was ever bubbling over with fun he was respected and obeyed by his children in the minutest particulars. His oldest daughter, Catherine, says of her father, "As to family government, it has been said that children love best those that govern them best. This was verified in our experience. Our mother was tender, gentle, and sympathizing; but all the discipline of government was with father. With most of his children, when quite young, he had one, two, or three seasons in which he taught them that obedience must be exact, prompt, and cheerful, and by a discipline so severe that it was thoroughly remembered and feared. Ever after, a decided word of command was all-sufficient. The obedience was to be speedy and without fretting or frowns. 'Mind your mother! Quick! No crying! Look pleasant!' These were words of command obeyed with almost military speed and precision."

Never was a father more idolized by his children than was Lyman Beecher. Mrs. Stowe mentions especially his power for exciting family enthusiasm. "Whenever he had a point to be carried, or work to be done, he would work the whole family up to a pitch of fervent zeal in which the strength of each seemed quadrupled. For instance, the wood for the family used to be brought in winter on ox-sleds, and piled up in the yard exactly over the spot where father wished to plant his cucumbers and melons. Of course as all this wood was to be cut and split and carried into the wood-house before the garden could be started, it required a miracle of generalship to get it done, considering the immense quantity of wood required to keep an old windy castle of a house comfortable in winter weather. The axes would ring and the chips fly; but jokes and stories would fly faster till all was cut and split. Then came the great work of wheeling in and piling."

Harriet would work like one possessed, sucked into the vortex of enthusiasm by her father's remarking, " I wish Harriet were a boy! She would do more than any of them!" Then would she throw aside her book or her needle and thread and, donning a little black coat which she thought made her look more like a boy, she would try to outdo all the rest till the wood was all in and the chips swept up. Frequently Doctor Beecher would raise a point of theology and start a discussion, taking the wrong or weaker side himself, to practice the youngsters in logic. If the children did not make good their side of the case, he would stop and explain to them the position and say, "The argument is thus and so! Now if you take this position you will be able to trip me up!" Thus he taught them to reason as if he had taught them to box or wrestle by actual face-to-face contest.

The task done, the Doctor always planned to have a great fishing expedition with the children. When Harriet was too little to go, she looked on these fishing expeditions as something pertaining only to her father and the older boys, and watched the busy preparations with regretful interest. They were all going to Great Pond and to Pine Island, to that wonderful blue pine forest that she could just see on the horizon, and who could tell what strange adventures they might meet!

When they were gone the house seemed so still and deserted all day long, — no singing, shouting, tramping, and wrestling of noisy, merry boys. Harriet would sit silent and lonely, sewing a long seam on a sheet by way of beguiling the time. At last it would begin to be dark, and the stars peeping out one by one would look down as if surprised to find a little girl who had gone to bed but not to sleep. With what joy she finally hailed in the distance the tramp of feet, the shouts and laughter of her father and brothers as, glad with triumph, they burst into the kitchen with long strings of perch, roach, pickerel, and bull-heads, with waving blades of sweet-flag and lofty heads of cat-tail, and pockets full of fragrant wintergreen, a generous portion of which was always bestowed upon her! To her eyes these were trophies from the dreamland of enchantment for which she had longed. She was then safe for an hour or more from being sent back to bed, and watched with delight the cheerful hurrying and scurrying to and fro, the waving of lights as the fish were cleaned in the back shed and the fire was kindled into a cheerful blaze, while her father stood over the frying-pan frying the fish. To his latest day Doctor Beecher was firm in the conviction that no feminine hand could fry fish with that perfection of skill which was his as a king of woodcraft and woodland cookery.

One of Harriet's favorite haunts was her father's study. It was an arched garret room, high above all the noise and confusion of the busy household, with a big window that commanded a view of Great Pond with its fringe of steel-blue pines. Its walls were set round from floor to ceiling with the quiet friendly faces of books, and there stood her father's study-chair and his writing-table, on which always lay open before him his Cruden's Concordance and the Bible. Here Harriet loved to retreat and curl herself up in a quiet corner with her favorite books around her. Here she had a restful, sheltered feeling as she thus sat and watched her father at his sermon-writing, turning his books and speaking to himself from time to time in a loud and earnest whisper. She vaguely felt that he was about some holy and mysterious work, far above her childish comprehension.

The books ranged around filled her too with solemn awe. There on the lower shelves were enormous folios, on whose backs she spelled in black letters " Lightfooti Opera," a title whereat she marveled, considering the bulk of the volumes. And overhead, grouped along in sociable rows, were books of all sizes and bindings, the titles of which she had read so often that she knew them by heart. There were Bell's "Sermons," Bonnett's "Inquiries," Bogue's "Essays," "Toplady on Predestination," "Boston's Fourfold State," Law's "Serious Call," and other works of the kind that she had looked over wistfully day after day, without finding even a hope of something interesting.

It was a happy hour for Harriet when her father brought home and set up in his bookcase Cotton Mather's "Magnalia." What wonderful stories these, and stories too about her own country, — stories that made her feel that the very ground under her feet was consecrated by some special dealings of God's wonder-working providence! When the good doctor related how a plague had wasted the Indian tribes, and so prepared a place for the Pilgrim Fathers to settle undisturbed, she felt in no wise doubtful of his application of the text, "He drave out the heathen and planted them." No Jewish maiden ever grew up with a more earnest faith that she belonged to a consecrated race, a people specially called and chosen of God for some great work on earth. Her faith in every word of the marvels related in this book was fully as great as the dear old credulous Doctor Mather could have desired. It filled her soul with a great eagerness to go forth and do some great and valiant deed for her God and her country. She wanted then, as always, to translate her feelings into deeds.

But aside from her father's study Harriet found poetry and romance in the various garrets and cellars of the old parsonage. There was, first, the garret over the kitchen, the floors of which in the fall were covered with stores of yellow pumpkins, fragrant heaps of quinces, and less fragrant piles of onions. There were bins of shelled corn and of oats, and, as in every other garret in the house, there were also barrels of old sermons and pamphlets.

But most stimulating to the imagination of a Puritan child, steeped in that wonderful allegory, Bunyan's "Pilgrim's Progress," was the smokehouse, which was a wide, deep chasm made in the kitchen chimney, in which the dried beef and the hams were prepared. The door which opened into this dismal recess glistened with condensed creosote, and Harriet trembled as she listened to an awful rumbling within, followed by crackling reverberations. One day she summoned courage to open the door and peep in, and was reminded of a passage in the " Pilgrim's Progress," which reads, "Then I saw in my dream that the shepherds had them to another place, in a bottom, where was a door in the side of a hill; and they opened the door and bid them look in.

"They looked in, therefore, and saw that within it was dark and smoky; they also thought that they heard a rumbling noise as of fire and a cry of some tormented, and they smelt the smell of brimstone."

Harriet closed the door and ran away trembling.

She delighted in upsetting the barrels of old sermons and pamphlets on the floor, pawing about in the contents, and reading with astonished eyes the queer titles. It seemed to her that there were thousands of unintelligible things. "An Appeal on the Unlawfulness of a Man's Marrying his Wife's Sister," turned up in every barrel she investigated. But — oh joy and triumph! one rainy day she found at the bottom of a barrel a copy of the " Arabian Nights "! Thenceforth her fortune was made. She had no idea of reading as is the fashion in these days— to read and dismiss a book. To read with her was a passion, and a book once read was read daily; becoming ever dearer as an old friend. The "Arabian Nights" transported her to far-off lands, and gave her a new world of her own. Thereafter, when things went wrong, when the boys went away to play higher than she dared climb in the barn, or started for fishing excursions, on which they considered her an encumbrance, she would find a snug corner, where, curled up in a quiet lair, she could at will sail forth into fairy-land on her bit of enchanted carpet.

It was also a great day when she discovered an old torn copy of the "Tempest." This experience she has wrought into that romance of the Maine coast, "The Pearl of Orr's Island," where she pictures Mara exploring the garret and finding in an old barrel of cast-off rubbish a bit of reading which she begged of her grandmother for her own. "It was the play of the 'Tempest,' torn from an old edition of Shakespeare, and was in that delightfully fragmentary condition that most particularly pleases children, because they conceive a mutilated treasure thus found to be more particularly their own property."

There was one class of tenants, whose presence and influence on Harriet's youthful mind must not be passed over. They were the rats. They had taken formal possession of the old parsonage, grown, multiplied, and become ancient in spite of traps, cats, or anything that could be devised against them. The family cat in Harriet's day, having taken a dispassionate survey of the situation, had given up the matter in despair and set herself philosophically to attending to other concerns. She selected a corner of the Doctor's study as her special domestic retreat. Here she made her lair on a heap of old pamphlets and sermons, whence, from time to time, she led forth litters of well-educated, orthodox kittens, who, like their mother, gazed on the rats with respectful curiosity, but ran no imprudent risks. Consequently the rats had, as it were, "the freedom of the city" in the old parsonage.

They romped all night on the floor of the garret over Harriet's sleeping-room, apparently busy hopping ears of corn across the floor and rolling them down into their nests between the beams. Sometimes she would hear them gnawing and sawing behind the wainscoting at the head of her bed as if they had set up a carpenter's shop there, and would be filled with terror lest they should come through into her bed. Then there were battles and skirmishes and squealings and fightings, and at times it would seem as if a whole detachment of rats rolled in an avalanche down the walls with the cobs of corn they had been stealing. When the mighty winds of the Litchfield winters were let loose and rumbled and thundered, roaring and tumbling down the chimneys, rattling the windows and doors; when the beams and rafters creaked and groaned like the timbers of a ship at sea, and the old house shook to its very foundations, then would the uproar among the rats grow louder and louder, and Harriet would dive under the bedclothes quaking with fear. Thus did the old parsonage exert its subtle influence, every day fashioning the sensitive, imaginative child.

Among Harriet's earliest recollections were those of a visit to Nutplains in Guilford, Connecticut, immediately after her mother's death. Her aunt Harriet Foote, for whom she was named, and who was with her mother during her sickness, brought her home to stay with her for a time. It was in Nutplains and Guilford that, little child that she was, she was deeply impressed by finding herself treated with a tenderness almost amounting to veneration by those who had known her mother.

Mrs. Stowe writes of this visit: "At Nutplains our mother lost to us seemed to live again. We saw her paintings, her needlework, and heard a thousand little doings and sayings of her daily life. And so dear was everything that belonged to grandmother and our Nutplains home, that the Episcopal service, even though not well read, was always chosen during our visits there in preference to our own. It seemed a part of Nutplains and the life there.

"There was also an interesting and well-selected library, and a portfolio of fine engravings; and, though the place was lonely, yet the cheerful hospitality that reigned there left it scarcely ever without agreeable visitors.

"I can now remember at the close of what seemed to me a long day's ride, arriving after dark at a lonely little white farmhouse, and being brought into a large parlor where a cheerful wood-fire was crackling, partly burned down into great heavy coals. I was placed in the arms of an old lady, who held me close and wept silently, a thing at which I marveled, for my great loss was already faded from my childish mind. But I could feel that this dear old grandmother received me with a heart full of love and sorrow. I recall still her bright white hair, the benign and tender expression of her venerable face, and the great gold ring she wore, which seemed so curious to my childish eyes. There was a little tea-table set out before the fire, and Uncle George came in from his farm-work, and sat down with grandma, and Aunt Harriet to tea.

"After supper I remember grandmother reading prayers, as was her custom, from a great prayerbook, which was her constant companion."

There were no amusements then specially provided for children. There were no children's books, and no Sunday-schools. It was a grown people's world, not a child's. Even the children's toys were so few and poor that, in comparison with our modern profusion, they could scarcely be said to exist. Harriet had toys, however, and her own playthings, as every child of lively fancy will. Childhood is poetic and creative, and can make to itself toys out of anything. She had the range of the great wood-pile in the back yard. She skipped, and climbed, and sang among its intricacies and found there treasures of wonder, —green velvet mosses, little white trees of lichen, long gray bearded mosses and fine scarlet cups, and fairy caps which she collected and cherished. With these she arranged landscapes in which green mosses made the fields, and little sprigs of spruce and ground-pine the trees, and bits of broken glass represented rivers and lakes, reflecting the overshadowing banks.

She had, too, hoards of chestnuts and walnuts that a squirrel might have envied, picked up with her own hands from under the autumn leaves; and — chief treasure of all — a wooden doll, with staring glass eyes, which was the central point of all her arrangements. To her she showed the chestnuts and walnuts, gave her the jay's feathers and the blue-bird's wing, — a trophy secured from the boys. She made her a bed of divers colors, and a set of tea-cups out of the backbone of a codfish; she brushed and curled her hair till she took all the curl out of it, and washed all the paint off her cheeks in motherly ablutions. This doll came to a tragic end. Harriet was awakened one morning by her little brother Charles calling out in the most cheerful voice imaginable, "0 Hattie, wake up! Henry and I have pulled your doll all to pieces!" To her dying day she carried the remembrance of the pang that went to her heart at these words.

There was probably no one who more profoundly influenced Mrs. Stowe's intellectual development than did her sea-faring uncle, Captain Samuel Foote. Of him her sister Catherine says, "After we removed to Litchfield, Uncle Samuel came among us, on his return from each voyage, as a sort of brilliant genius of another sphere, bringing gifts and wonders that seemed to wake up new faculties in all. Sometimes he came from the shores of Spain, with mementoes of the Alhambra and the ancient Moors; sometimes from Africa, bringing Oriental caps or Moorish slippers; sometimes from South America, with ingots of silver or strange implements from the tombs of the Incas, or hammocks wrought by South American tribes of Indians.

"He was a man of great practical common sense, united with large ideality, a cultivated taste and very extensive reading. With this was combined a humorous combativeness, that led him to attack the special theories and prejudices of his friends, sometimes jocosely and sometimes in earnest.

"Of course he and father were in continual good-natured skirmishes, in which all the New England peculiarities of theology and of character were held up, both in caricature and in sober verity.

"I remember long discussions in which he maintained that Turks were more honest than Christians, bringing very startling facts in evidence. Then I heard his serious tales of Roman Catholic bishops and archbishops whom he had carried to and from Spain and America, and he affirmed them to be as learned and as truly pious and devoted to the good of men as any Protestant to be found in America.

"The new fields of vision presented by my uncle, the skill and adroitness of his arguments, the array of his facts, combined to tax my father's powers to the utmost.

"Whenever Uncle Sam came to Litchfield he brought a stock of new books which he and Aunt Mary read aloud. This was the time when Scott, Byron, Moore, and that great galaxy of contemporary writers were issuing their works at intervals of only a few months, all of which were read and re-read in the family circle."

When Harriet was between six and seven years old, her father married Miss Harriet Porter, of Portland, Maine. She has herself thus described the advent of the new mother: "I was about six years old and slept in the nursery with my two younger brothers. We knew father was gone away somewhere on a journey, and was expected home, and thus the sound of a bustle or disturbance in the house more easily awoke us. We heard father's voice in the entry, and started up, crying out as he entered our room,'Why, here's pa!' A cheerful voice called out from behind him,' And here's ma!'

"A beautiful lady, very fair, with bright blue eyes, and soft auburn hair bound round with a black velvet bandeau, came into the room, smiling, eager, and happy-looking, and, coming up to our beds, kissed us, and told us that she loved little children and would be our mother. We wanted forthwith to get up and be dressed; but she pacified us

with the promise that we should find her in the morning.

"Never did mother-in-law make prettier or sweeter impression. The next morning I remember we looked at her with awe. She seemed to us so fair, so elegant, so delicate that we were afraid to go near her. We must have been rough, redcheeked, hearty country children, honest, obedient, and bashful. She was peculiarly dainty and neat in all her ways and arrangements; I remember I used to feel breezy, rough, and rude in her presence. We felt a little in awe of her, as if she were a strange princess, rather than our own mamma; but her voice was very sweet, her ways of moving and speaking very graceful, and she took us up in her lap and let us play with her beautiful f hands, which seemed like wonderful things made of pearl and ornamented with rings."

Once in a fit of delirious boldness Harriet marched up to her, and putting her little hands behind her back, and thrusting her head somewhat forward, said defiantly, "You have come and married my pa! and when I grow up I will go and marry your pa!"

One Sunday evening, shortly after the arrival of the new mother, Doctor Beecher, who was at that time given to an undiscriminating admiration for the works of the great Jonathan Edwards, was reading to her from a volume of sermons by that great divine. It happened to be the sermon with the pungent title," Sinners in the Hands of an Angry God." Harriet was curled up on the sofa, apparently absorbed in a book of her own. Drawn to observe closely her new mother, she saw that she seemed to be listening with abhorrence and suppressed emotion. A bright red spot suffused each cheek, every moment growing brighter and redder. Finally rising to her stately height, she swept out of the room, saying as she went, "Mr. Beecher, I will not listen to another word! Why, it is horrible! It is a slander on the character of my Heavenly Father!" Harriet was impressed with the stupefaction pictured on her father's face. If a bucket of ice-water had been thrown over him, the effect could not have been

more startling. He probably never again read Edwards's lurid pages with the same ease of mind as formerly. Doubtless this incident placed his foot on the first rung of a ladder which the ultra-orthodox of the period thought led anywhere but to heaven. Harriet Porter, though orthodox was human, and she belonged to a different age from Edwards.

Harriet attended a school for young women kept by a Miss Sarah Pierce, who is described as a woman of " more than ordinary talent, sprightly in conversation, social, and full of benevolent activity." In process of time the school was enlarged and her nephew, Mr. John Brace, became her assistant. Of him Mrs. Stowe writes: "Mr. Brace was one of the most stimulating and inspiring instructors that I ever knew. He was himself widely informed, an enthusiast in botany, mineralogy, and the natural sciences generally. The constant conversation that he kept up on these subjects tended more to develop the mind and inspire a love of literature than any mere routine studies could do.

"This school was the only one I ever knew that carried out a thorough course of ancient and modera history.... The interest of these historical recitations, with a preceptor so widely informed and so fascinating in conversation as Mr. Brace, extended further than the class. Much of the training and inspiration of my early days consisted, not in the things I was supposed to be studying, but in hearing, while seated unnoticed at my desk, the conversation of Mr. Brace with the older classes. There from hour to hour I listened to historical criticisms and discussions, or to recitations in such works as Paley's 'Moral Philosophy,' Blair's 'rhetoric,' Alison 'On Taste,' all full of most awakening suggestions to my thoughts.

"Mr. Brace exceeded all the instructors that I ever knew in the faculty of teaching the art of English composition. The constant excitement in which he kept the minds of his pupils — the wide and varied regions of thought into which he led them —formed a preparation for teaching composition, the main requisite for which, whatever people may think, is to have something that one feels interested to say.

"His manner was to divide his school of about one hundred pupils into divisions of about three or four, one of which was to write every week. At the same time he inspired an ambition to write by calling every week for volunteers, and every week there were those who volunteered to write.

"I remember I could have been but nine years old, and my handwriting hardly formed, when the enthusiasm he inspired led me, greatly to his amusement, I believe, to volunteer to write every week. The first week the subject of the composition chosen by the class was, 'The Difference between the Natural and the Moral Sublime.'

"One may smile at this for a child nine years of age; but it is the best account I can give of his manner of teaching to say that the discussion that he had held in the class not only made me understand the subject as thoroughly as I do now, but so excited me that I felt sure that I had something to say about it; and that first composition with half the words misspelled amused him greatly.

"By two years of constant practice, under his training and suggestion, I had gained so far as to be appointed one of the writers for the annual exhibition, a proud distinction as I then viewed it. The subject assigned me was one that had been very fully discussed in the school in a manner to show to the best advantage Mr. Brace's peculiarity in awakening the minds of his pupils to the higher regions of thought. The question was, 'Can the Immortality of the Soul be Proved by the Light of Nature?'

"Several of theyoung ladies had written strongly in the affirmative. Mr. Brace himself had written in the negative. To all these compositions and subsequent discussions I had listened, and, in view of them, chose to adopt the negative.

"I remember the scene at that exhibition to me so eventful. The hall was crowded with all the literati of Litchfield. Before them all our compositions were read aloud. When mine was read

I noticed that father, who was sitting on high by Mr. Brace, brightened, and looked interested, and at the close I heard him ask, Who wrote that composition?' 'Your Daughter, Sir!' was the answer. It was the proudest moment of my life. There was no mistaking father's face when he was pleased, and to have interested him was past all juvenile triumphs."

"Never shall I forget the dignity and sense of importance which swelled my mind when I was first pronounced old enough to go to meeting," writes Mrs. Stowe in another account of those early Litchfield days.

"To my childish eyes our old meeting-house was an awe-inspiring place. To me it seemed fashioned very nearly on the model of Noah's ark and Solomon's Temple, as set forth in the pictures of my scripture catechism—pictures which I did not doubt were authentic copies; and what more respectable and venerable architectural precedent could any one desire? Its double rows of windows of which I knew the number by heart, its doors with great wooden curls over them, its belfry projecting out of the east end, its steeple and bell, all inspired as much sense of the sublime in me as Strasburg Cathedral itself; and the inside was not a whit less imposing. How magnificent to my eye seemed the turnip-like canopy that hung over the minister's head, hooked by a long iron rod to the wall above! How apprehensively did I consider the question, what would become of him if it should fall. With what amazement I gazed on the panels on either side of the pulpit, in each of which was carved and painted a flaming red tulip, bolt upright, with its leaves projecting out at right angles. Then there was a grapevine, basso-relievo in front, with its exactly triangular bunches of grapes, alternating at exact intervals with exactly triangular leaves.

"To me it was a faultless representation of how grapevines ought to look, if they would only be straight and regular, instead of curling and scrambling, and twisting themselves into all sorts of uncanny shapes.

"It was good orthodox custom of old times to take every part of the domestic establishment to meeting, even down to the faithful dog, who as he had supervised the labors of the week, also came with due particularity to supervise the worship on Sunday. I think I can see now the fitting out on a Sunday morning — the one wagon, or two, as the case might be, tackled up with an 'old gray,' or 'old bay,' with a buffalo skin thrown over the seat by way of a cushion, and all the family in their Sunday best packed in for meeting; while waiting Bose, Watch, or Towser stood to be an outguard, and went meekly pattering up hill and down dale behind the wagon.

"Arrived at meeting the canine part of the establishment generally conducted themselves with great decorum, lying down and going to sleep as decently as anybody present, except when some mischief-loving flies would make a sortie on them, when you might hear the snap of their jaws as they vainly tried to lay hold upon the intruder.

"Now and then, between some of the sixthlies, seventhlies, and eighthlies of the long sermon, you might hear some old patriarch of a dog giving himself a rousing shake, and pitpatting soberly up and down the broad aisle as if to see that everything was going properly, after which he would lie down and compose himself to sleep again. This was certainly as improving a way of spending Sunday as a good Christian dog could desire.

"We are compelled to acknowledge that Trip, the minister's dog, did not always conduct himself with that propriety and decorum that befitted his social station and responsible position. He was emotional and nervous, and never could be taught to respect conventionalities. If anything about the performance in the singers' seat did not please him he was apt to express himself in a lugubrious howl. If the sermon was longer than suited him, he would gape with such a loud creak of his jaws as would arouse everybody's attention. If flies disturbed his afternoon naps, he would give sudden snarls or snaps; or if he had troubled dreams, he would bark out in his sleep in a manner not only to interrupt his own slumbers, but those of worthy deacons and old ladies, whose sanctuary repose was thereby sorely broken up and troubled. For these reasons Trip had been denied the sanctuary privileges usually accorded to good dogs of the period. He was shut up on Sunday for private meditation. Trip of course was only the more strongly bent on social worship with dogs and men. He would hide behind doors, jump out of windows, sneak through byways and alleys, and lie hid till the second bell had done tolling, and then patter up the broad aisle, innocent and happy, and take his position right under the pulpit and in front of the minister's pew.

"One Sunday Doctor Beecher exchanged with the Rev. Father Mills of Torringford. He was a thin, wiry, frisky little man, in a powdered white wig, black tights, and silk stockings, with bright knee-buckles and shoe-buckles; with round, dark snapping eyes; and a curious high, cracked, squeaking voice, the very first tones of which made all the children stare and giggle.

"On the Sunday morning when the event we are about to relate transpired, we children went to the house of the Lord in a very hilarious state, all ready to explode with laughter on the slightest provocation.

"The occasion was not long wanting. Directly after the closing notes of the tolling bell, Master Trip walked soberly up the centre aisle and seating himself gravely in front of the pulpit, raised his nose critically and expectantly towards the scene of the forthcoming performance. He wore an alert, attentive air that befitted a soundly orthodox dog that scents a possible heresy, and deems it his sacred duty to narrowly watch the performance.

"He evidently felt called upon to see who and what were to occupy that pulpit in his master's absence. Up rose Father Mills, and up went Trip's nose vibrating with attention. The good man began to read the opening hymn: —
'Sing to the Lord aloud,' when Trip broke into a dismal howl.

"Father Mills went on to give directions to the deacons to remove the dog in the same tone in which he read the hymn, so that the effect of the whole performance was somewhat as follows: —

'Sing to the Lord aloud, (please put that dog out!) And make a joyful noise.'

"We youngsters were delivered over to the temptations of Satan and sank in waves and billows of hysterical giggles while Trip was put out and the choir did its best at making a 'joyful noise.'"

In front of the pulpit was a bench on which at noon between the two long sermons some members of the congregation who came from afar sat and ate their dinners. Consequently there would be by time of the afternoon service sundry crumbs of cheese and bread on the floor. In the base of the pulpit just above the floor dwelt a number of pious church mice, and in the afternoons when Doctor Beecher was thundering away in the lofty pulpit, Harriet would see their little bright eyes shining cautiously out of their holes. If the doctor became quieter they would venture out and begin a meal on the crumbs; but suddenly some awful words, like reprobation or foreordination, would come roaring down from above, and the mice would run for their lives, and not venture out again till they thought the danger past.

Harriet had hallowed as well as humorous associations connected with the thought of the old church. "One beautiful, fresh, dewy, summer morning, when it seemed as if all nature were hushed and listening for the music of higher spheres," she stood at her open window looking out on the green hills opposite, the stately trees feathered with their varied greens, and the meadows waving with buttercups and daisies. On the old apple tree under her window, a bobolink was tilting up and down chattering and singing with all his might. Early that morning she had been reminded that it was Sunday, the holy Sabbath day, by this incident. Her two younger brothers, Henry and Charles, slept together in a little trundle-bed in a corner of the nursery where she also slept. She was waked

by the two little fellows chattering to one another, while they lay in their bed making little sheep out of the cotton pulled from the holes in the old quilt that covered them, and pasturing them on the undulating hillsides and meadows which their imaginations conjured up amid the bedclothes. Suddenly Charles's eyes grew big with fright and he cried out, "Henry, this is wicked! It's Sunday!" There was a moment of consternation, followed by silence, as both little curly heads disappeared under the old coverlid.

Yes, it was Sunday, and Harriet was trying her best to feel herself a dreadful sinner, but with very poor success. She was so healthy and the blood raced and tingled so in her young veins. She tried to feel her sins and count them up, but the birds, and the daisies, and the buttercups were a constant interruption, and she went into the old meeting-house quite dissatisfied with herself. When she saw the white cloth, the shining cups, and the snowy bread of the Communion Table, she hopelessly felt that the service could have nothing for a little girl,—it would be all for the grown-up people, the initiated Christians. Nevertheless, when her father began to speak she was drawn to listen by a sort of pathetic earnestness in his voice.

The Doctor was feeling very deeply, and he had chosen for his text, the declaration of Jesus: "I call you not servants, but friends." His subject was Jesus as the soul-friend offered to every human being. Forgetting his doctrinal subtleties, he spoke with the simplicity and tenderness of a rich nature concerning the faithful, generous love of Christ. Deep feeling inclined to simplicity of language, and Doctor Beecher spoke in words that even a child could understand. Harriet sat absorbed, her large blue eyes gathered tears as she listened, and when the Doctor said, " Come, then, and trust your soul to this faithful friend," her little heart throbbed, "I will!"

She sat through the Sacramental service that followed with swelling heart and tearful eyes, and walked home filled with a new joy. She went up into her father's study and threw herself into his arms, saying, "Father, I have given myself to Jesus and he has taken me. " He held her silently to his heart for a moment, and she felt his tears dropping on her head. "Is it so?" he said, "then has a new flower blossomed in the Kingdom this day." CHAPTER II ON THE THRESHOLD

Harriet was between twelve and thirteen when she came to Hartford, Connecticut, to attend a school recently established by her sister Catherine. The schoolroom was over a harness store, which, after the fashion of the day, had for a sign two white horses. Great was the surprise and pleasure with which Harriet gazed upon this triumph of artistic skill as it then appeared to her. One of the young men who worked in the harness shop in the rear of the store had a fine tenor voice, and often delighted her by singing in school hours: —

"When in cold oblivion's shade,
Beauty, wealth, and power are laid,
When around the sculptured shrine,
Moss shall cling, and ivy twine
Where immortal spirits reign,
There shall we all meet again."

The expense of her board was provided for by a kind of exchange common in those days. Mr. Isaac D. Bull, of Hartford, sent a daughter to Miss Pierce's school in Litchfield, who boarded in Doctor Beecher's family in exchange for Harriet's board in his own. The very soul of neatness and order pervaded the whole establishment, and Mrs. Stowe has said that her own good, refined, particular stepmother could not have found a family better suited to her taste had she searched the whole town. Mr. Bull, "a fine vigorous man on the declining slope of life, but full of energy and kindness," kept a large wholesale drug store, and his oldest son had established a retail drug store of his own at the sign of the Good Samaritan. Harriet frequently contemplated with reverence a large picture of the Good Samaritan relieving the wounded traveler, which formed a conspicuous part of this sign.

Harriet occupied a little hall bedroom which looked out over the Connecticut River. Mrs. Bull took her young boarder into her heart as well as into her house. If Harriet was sick, nothing could exceed her watchful care and tender nursing. The daughter, Miss Mary Ann Bull, was a beauty of local celebrity, with long raven curls falling from a comb on the top of her head. She had a rich soprano voice and was one of the leading singers in the choir of the Congregational Church. She received frequent and impressive calls from a solemn young man who lived next door. The three brothers were also singers, and the family circle was often enlivened by quartette-singing and fluteplaying.

In Hartford Harriet found what she had long craved, real and lasting friendships with girls of her own age. One of these friends was Catherine Cogswell, a daughter of Hartford's leading physician. The other was Georgiana May. Georgiana had two younger sisters and a number of brothers. She was older and more sedate than Catherine, and consequently less attractive to the other girls, but the friendship that sprang up between her and Harriet endured undimmed through life. Mrs. Stowe has described Catherine Cogswell as "one of the most sunny-tempered, amiable, lovable, and sprightly souls she had ever known." Her companionship was so much in demand that it was difficult for Harriet to see much of her. Her time was all bespoken by the various girls who wanted to walk to or from school with her, and at the halfhour recess Harriet was only one of the many suppliants at her shrine. Yet among the many claimants there was always a little place kept here and there for Hattie Beecher. Catherine and Georgiana were reading Virgil when Harriet entered the school and began the study of Latin, but by the end of the first year she had made a translation of Ovid into verse that was so creditable as to be read at the final exhibition of the school.

Harriet was, at this time, much interested in poetry, and it was her dream to be a poet. Consequently, she began to write a metrical drama which she called "Cleon." Cleon was a Greek lord residing at the court of the Emperor Nero, who after much searching, doubting, and tribulation became a convert to Christianity. This theme filled her thoughts sleeping and waking, and blank book after blank book bore testimony to her industry, till finally her sister Catherine pounced upon her and declared that she must not waste her time trying to write poetry, but must discipline her mind by the study of Butler's " Analogy." Young as she was, she was set to instructing a class of girls as oldas herself in the " Analogy "; a task for which she had been fitted by listening to Mr. Brace's lectures at the Litchfield school. She wrote out abstracts of the " Analogy," and mastered chapter after chapter just ahead of her pupils. This she did in addition to her regular work as a pupil in the school. From then on she became both pupil and teacher.

At this period, too, she read for the first time Baxter's " Saints' Everlasting Rest," and she often said that no book ever affected her more powerfully. As she walked the pavements she wished that they might sink beneath her, and she awake in heaven.

Among her manifold duties was the instruction of her jolly, little, round-faced brother, Henry Ward. One time in desperation she said, "Now, Henry, please do stop your fun and attend to your grammar lesson! Now, Henry, listen! His is the possessive pronoun. You would not say him book; you would say his book."

"Why can't I say himbook, sister Hattie? I say hymnbook every Sunday." This sally quite destroyed the gravity of the exasperated little teacher.

Shortly after going to Hartford Harriet made a call upon the Rev. Dr. Hawes, her father's friend, and her spiritual adviser, which left an enduring impression upon her mind. It was her father's advice that she join the church in Hartford, as he had received a call to Boston, and the breaking up of the Litchfield home was imminent. Accordingly, accompanied by her two school friends, she went one day to the pastor's study to consult him concerning the contemplated step. In those days much stress was placed on religious experience, and more especially on what was termed a conviction of sin, and self-examination was carried to an extreme calculated to drive to desperation a sensitive, high-strung nature. The good man listened to the child's simple and modest statement of her Christian experience, and then with an awful though kindly solemnity of speech and manner, said, "Harriet! do you feel that if the universe should be destroyed (alarming pause) you could be happy with God alone?" After struggling in vain to fix in her mind the meaning of the sounds which fell on her ears like the measured tolling of a funeral bell, the child of fourteen stammered out, "Yes, sir!"

"You realize, I trust, in some measure, at least, the deceitfulness of your own heart, and that in punishment for your sins God might justly leave you to make yourself as miserable as you have made yourself sinful."

Having thus effectually, and to his own satisfaction, fixed the child's attention on the morbid and over-sensitive workings of her own heart, the good, and truly kind-hearted man dismissed her with a fatherly benediction. He had been alarmed at her simple and natural way of entering the Kingdom. It was not theologically sound to make short cuts to salvation. The child went into the conference full of peace and joy, and she came out full of distress and misgivings, but the good Doctor had done his duty as he saw it.

It was a theological age, and in the Beecher family theology was the supreme interest. It fills their letters as it filled their lives. Not only was the age theological, but transitional, and characterized by intense intellectual activity, accompanied by emotional excitement. The winds of doctrine were let loose, blowing first from this quarter and then from that. Doctor Beecher spent his days in weathering theological cyclones, but the worst of all arose in his own family, among his own children. Great as were his intellectual powers he was no match for his daughter Catherine and his son Edward, — the metaphysical Titans who sprang from his own loins. It was almost in a tone of despair that this theological Samuel, who had

hewn so many heretical Agags in pieces before the Lord, wrote concerning his own daughter: "Catherine's letter will disclose the awfully interesting state of her mind.... You perceive she is now handling edged tools with powerful grasp.... I have at times been at my wits' end to know what to do.... I conclude that nothing safe can be done, but to assert ability and obligation and guilt upon divine authority, throwing in at the same time as much collateral light from reason as the case admits of." Catherine was at this time breaking out of the prison-house of the traditional orthodoxy, and her brother Edward was in many ways in sympathy with her, though not as radical as she. Doctor Beecher was contending with might and main for the traditional Calvinism, and yet in his zeal for its defense he often took positions that surprised and alarmed his brother ministers, seriously disturbed their dogmatic slumbers, and caused them grave doubts as to his orthodoxy. So

"Cannon to right of them,
Cannon to left of them,...
Volley'd and thunder'd."

Harriet, keenly alive and morbidly sensitive to the spiritual atmosphere in which she was compelled to live, was driven nearly distracted by the strife of tongues and division of opinion among those to whom she looked for counsel and for guidance.

The events of family history that led to this situation, so decisive in its influence on Harriet's mental development and subsequent literary activity, were as follows. When Harriet was in her eleventh year her sister Catherine had become engaged to Professor Alexander Fisher of Yale College. He was a young man of brilliant talents, and especially noted for his mathematical genius. As an undergraduate at Yale he distinguished himself by original and valuable contributions to mathematical astronomy. Immediately on graduation he was appointed a professor of mathematics, and sent abroad by his alma mater to devote some time to study and the purchase of books and mathematical instruments. The ship Albion, on which

he sailed, was wrecked on a reef off the coast of Ireland. Of the twenty-three cabin passengers only one reached the shore. He was a man of great physical strength, and all night long clung to the jagged rocks at the foot of the cliff, against which the sea broke, till ropes were lowered down from above, and he was drawn up limp and exhausted. He often told of the calm bravery with which Professor Fisher met his end.

Up to this time in her life Catherine had been noted for the gayety of her spirits and the brilliancy of her mind. An inimitable story-teller and a great mimic, it seemed her aim to keep every one laughing. Her versatile mind and ready wit enabled her to pass brilliantly through her school days with comparatively little mental exertion, and before she was twenty-one she had become a teacher in a school for girls in New London, Connecticut. It was about this time that she met Professor Fisher, and they soon became engaged. When the news of his death reached her, to the crushing of earthly hopes and plans was added an agony of apprehension for his soul. He had never been formally converted; and hence, by the teachings of the times, his soul as well as his body was lost. She writes to her brother Edward: "It is not so much ruined hopes of this life, it is dismay and apprehension for his immortal spirit. Oh, Edward, where is he now? Are the noble faculties of such a mind doomed to everlasting woe?" Anxiously, but in vain, she searched his letters and journals for something on which she might build a hope of his eternal welfare. "Mournful contemplations awakened when I learned more of the mental exercises of him I mourned, whose destiny was forever fixed, alas, I know not where! I learned from his letters, and in other ways, as much as I could have learned from his diary. I found that, even from early childhood, he had ever been uncommonly correct and conscientious, so that his parents and family could scarcely remember of his doing anything wrong, so far as relates to outward conduct; and year after year, with persevering and unexampled effort, he sought to yield that homage of the heart to his Maker which was required, but he could not; like the friend who followed his steps he had no strength.... It seemed to me that my lost friend had done all that unassisted human strength could do; and often the dreadful thought came to me that all was in vain, and that he was wailing that he ever had been born in that dark world where hope never comes, and that I was following his steps to that dreadful scene."

So she struggled on in the grasp of that New England Calvinism which her own father preached. Once she wrote to him, "I feel as Job did, that I could curse the day in which I was born. I wonder that Christians who realize the worth of immortal souls should be willing to give life to immortal minds to be placed in such a dreadful world." The letters which Doctor Beecher wrote to her at this time were considered a very able defense of New England Calvinism, but they did not satisfy her. It may be doubted if they even satisfied him, or if he from this time ever rested with the same serenity of mind on the traditional foundations. It was an epoch in the history of the Beecher family, and in the history of the New England theology. It was in this event of family history that both Edward Beecher's "Conflict of Ages" and Mrs. Stowe's "Minister's Wooing" found their peculiar inspiration. It is certain that, without this tragedy, neither of these works, so influential in determining the current of religious thought in America, would have been written.

Miss Beecher passed the two years following the death of Professor Fisher at Franklin, Massachusetts, at the home of his parents, where she listened to the fearless and pitiless Calvinism of Doctor Nathaniel Emmons. Her mind was too strong and buoyant to be overwhelmed and crushed by an experience that would have driven a weaker and less resolute nature to insanity. Not finding herself able to love a God whom she had been taught to look upon, to use her own language," as a perfectly happy being unmoved by my sorrows or my tears, and looking upon me only

with dislike and aversion," and gifted naturally with a capacity for close metaphysical analysis and a robust fearlessness in following her premises to logical conclusions, she arrived at results which, if not always of permanent value, were certainly startling and original.

The conventional New England Calvinism gave her no satisfactory solution for her difficulties. She was tormented with doubts. "What has the Son of God done which the meanest and most selfish creature upon earth would not have done?" she asked herself. "After making such a wretched race and placing them in such disastrous circumstances, somehow, without any sorrow or trouble, Jesus Christ had a human nature that suffered and died. If something else besides ourselves will do all the suffering, who would not save millions of wretched beings, and receive all the honor and gratitude without any of the trouble?" Yet when such thoughts passed through her mind she felt that it was "all pride, rebellion, and sin." So she struggled on, sometimes floundering deep in the mire of doubt, and then lifted out of it by her constitutionally buoyant spirits.

It was in this condition of mind that she came to Hartford in the winter of 1824 and opened her school. In the practical experience of teaching she found at last the solution of her troubles. Turning aside from doctrinal difficulties and theological quagmires, she determined " to find happiness in living to do good." She says: "It was right to pray and read the Bible, and so I prayed and read the Bible. It was right to try to save others, and so I tried to save them. In all these years I never had any fear of punishment or hope of reward."

Without ever having heard of pragmatism, she became a kind of pragmatist. She continues: "After two or three years I commenced giving instruction in mental philosophy, and at the same time began a regular course of lectures and instructions from the Bible and was much occupied with plans for governing my school, and in devising means to lead my pupils to become obedient, amiable, and pious." These "means" re-

sulted in a code of principles for the government of her school which were nothing more nor less than carefully formulated common sense with plenty of the "milk of human kindness" thrown in. These principles she carefully compared with the government of God, and came to the conclusion that He in his infinitely mighty and complex task of governing the universe was applying the same fundamental principles as she in the relatively infinitesimal and simple task of governing her school. This was her solution, and this the view of the divine nature that was for so many years preached by her brother Henry Ward, and set forth in the writings of her sister Harriet.

Harriet and Henry Ward took this position with their hearts, and held it with their heads. They ever felt their way with their hearts and followed with their intellects. The reverse was true of Edward and Catherine. They were the great metaphysicians of the family. Doctor Beecher presented just the inconsistent mingling of the two kinds of mental process which one might expect in the father of such children. It was said of him that he was the father of more brains than any other man in America. It might with equal truth have been said that he was the father of more heart than any other man in America. The view of God as manifested in Jesus Christ, which came to Catherine Beecher as the solution of her difficulties by long mental struggle, was essentially the same that came to Harriet by intuition as a child of thirteen in the old meeting-house at Litchfield. It was truly religious, non-theological, and practical. But because it was non-theological they were not to be permitted to rest in it peacefully.

In March, 1826, Doctor Beecher, having resigned his pastorate in Litchfield, accepted a call to the Hanover Street Church in Boston. In making this change he was actuated partly by personal motives, his salary in Litchfield being inadequate to the support of his large family, and partly by the great strategic importance of the Boston church in the war against Unitarianism.

In Boston his preaching, which has been called "logic on fire," became more aggressively theological than it had ever been before. He felt that God had placed him there to fight and crush a soul-destroying heresy. The stake was nothing so paltry as power and empire, or even human lives. It was the immortal souls of men. Now, although Mrs. Stowe's loyal soul would never have acknowledged that her father's preaching acted unfavorably on her mental development, such was unmistakably the case. The atmosphere of mental excitement and conflict in which her father lived and preached at this time drove her already over-stimulated mind to the point of distraction. Too much mental strain and too little exercise had brought her to her seventeenth year without the strength which should have been the heritage of her robust childhood.

In February, 1827, her sister Catherine writes to her father: "I have received some letters from Harriet to-day which make me feel uneasy. She says, 'I don't know that I am fit for anything and I have thought that I could wish to die young, and let the remembrance of me and my faults perish in the grave rather than live, as I fear I do, a trouble to every one. You don't know how perfectly wretched I often feel; so useless, so weak, so destitute of all energy. Mamma often tells me that I am a strange, inconsistent being. Sometimes I could not sleep and have groaned and cried till midnight, while in the day-time I have tried to appear cheerful, and have succeeded so well that Papa has reproved me for laughing so much, I was so absent sometimes that I made strange mistakes, and then they all laughed at me, and I laughed too, though I felt I should go distracted. I wrote rules, made out a regular system for dividing my time; but my feelings vary so much that it is almost impossible for me to be regular.'" Catherine also writes to her brother Edward that she thinks it the best thing for Harriet to return to Hartford where she can talk freely with her. "I can get her books," continues Catherine, "and Catherine Cogswell and Georgiana May, and her friends here can do

more for her than any one in Boston, for they love her and she loves them very much.... Harriet will have young society here all the time, which she cannot have at home, and I think cheerful and amusing friends will do much for her. I can do better in preparing her to teach drawing than any one else, for I know best what is needed."

The result was that Harriet returned to Hartford where she passed a month or so and then in the spring went with her friend Georgiana May to visit Nutplains, in Guilford, which, as we have already learned, was dear to her from childhood. The August following her visit to Guilford she writes to her brother Edward in a strain that reveals a state of mind bordering on religious melancholy, but at the same time shows that she is returning to mental health and cheerfulness. "Many of my objections you did remove that afternoon we spent together. After that I was not as unhappy as I had been. I felt, nevertheless, that my views were very indistinct and contradictory, and feared that if you left me thus, I might return to the same dark desolate state in which I had been all summer. I felt that my immortal interest for both worlds was depending on the turn my feelings might take. In my disappointment and distress I called upon God, and it seemed as if I was heard. I felt that He could supply the loss of all earthly love. All misery and darkness were over. I felt as if restored, never more to fall. Such sober certainty of waking bliss had long been a stranger to me. But even then I had doubts as to whether these feelings were right, because I felt love to God alone without that ardent love to my fellow creatures that Christians have often felt.... I cannot say what it is makes me reluctant to speak of my feelings. It costs me an effort to express feeling of any kind, but more particularly to speak of my private religious feelings. If any one questions me my first impulse is to conceal all I can. As for expression of affection towards my brothers and sisters, and companions and friends, the stronger the affection the less inclinedtion I have to express it. Yet sometimes I think myself

the most frank, communicative, and open of all beings, and at other times the most reserved. If you can resolve all my caprices into general principles you will do more than I can. Your speaking so much philosophically has a tendency to repress confidence. We never wish to have our feelings analyzed down, and every little nothing that we say brought to the test of mathematical demonstration.

"It appears to me that if I could only adopt the views of God you presented to my mind they would exert a strong and beneficial influence over my character. But I am afraid to accept them for several reasons. First, it seems to be taking from the majesty and dignity of the divine character to suppose that his happiness can be at all affected by the conduct of his sinful, erring creatures. Secondly, it seems to me that such views of God would have an effect on our own minds in lessening that reverence and fear which is one of the greatest motives to us for action. For, although to a generous mind the thought of the love of God would be a sufficient incentive to action, there are times of coldness when that love is not felt, and then there remains no sort of stimulus. I find as I adopt these sentiments I feel less fear of God, and, in view of sin, I feel only a sensation of grief which is more easily dispelled and forgotten than that I formerly felt." This letter shows how she was driven hither and thither by the powerful and somewhat contradictory influences brought to bear upon her mind by her father, her brother Edward, and her sister Catherine. She is naturally drawn to the winning and restful conception of God as like Jesus Christ which both her brother Edward and her sister Catherine unite in presenting to her, but at the same time she shows how the iron of her father's Calvinism has passed into her soul. It may make her very unhappy and depressed, but still she cannot let it go immediately. For dull, lethargic souls Calvinism may be a most excellent tonic under given conditions, but on her artistic and sensitive nature it acted like a subtle poison. It appealed to her reason and left her heart unsatisfied, — nay, even wounded and bleeding. She is drawn hither and thither by conflicting tendencies within herself. Again she writes to Edward and unconsciously paraphrasing a saying of Fe'nelon, remarks: "It is only to the most perfect Being in the universe that imperfection can look and hope for patience. You do not know how harsh and forbidding everything seems compared with his character! All through the day in my intercourse with others, everything seems to have a tendency to destroy the calmness of mind gained by communion with Him. One flatters me, another is angry with me, another is unjust to me. . "You speak of your predilection for literature having been a snare to you. I have found it so myself. I can scarcely think without tears and indignation, that all that is beautiful, lovely, and poetic, has been laid on other altars. Oh, will there never be a poet with a heart enlarged and purified by the Holy Spirit, who shall throw all the graces of harmony, all the enchantments of feeling, pathos, and poetry, around sentiments worthy of them?... It matters little what service he has for me... I do not mean to live in vain. He has given me talents and I will lay them at his feet well satisfied if He will accept them."

This rhapsodical, overstrained state of mind was highly characteristic of this period of her life. The high tension was naturally followed by seasons of depression and gloom.

During the winter of 1829 she is in Hartford again assisting her sister Catherine in the school. She writes to her brother Edward, "Little things have great power over me, and if I meet with the least thing that crosses my feelings, I am often rendered unhappy for days and weeks. I wish I could bring myself to feel perfectly indifferent to the opinions of others. I believe that there never was a person more dependent on the good and evil opinions of those around than I am!" This despair is inevitable to one earnestly seeking the truth as she was, amid conflicting counsels. She is now eighteen, but still morbidly introspective, sensitive, and overwrought.

She apparently lives largely in her emotions. In closing one of her letters she says, "This desire to be loved forms, I fear, the great motive for all my actions. " Again she writes to her brother Edward, "I have been carefully reading the book of Job, and I do not find in it the views of God you have presented to me. God seems to have stripped a dependent creature of all that renders life desirable, and then to have answered his complaints from the whirlwind; and,instead of showing mercy and pity, to have overwhelmed him by a display of his justice. From the view of God that I received from you, I should have expected that a being that sympathizes with his guilty, afflicted creatures would not have spoken thus. Yet, after all, I do believe that God is such a being as you represent him to be, and in the New Testament I find in the character of Jesus Christ a revelation of God as merciful and compassionate; in fact, just such a God as I need!" This was the vision of God that came to her at the time of her conversion. It was the confusing and perturbing influence of her father's Calvinistic theology that had dimmed that gracious vision. Out of the prisonhouse of Giant Despair she had been delivered by the teachings of her sister Catherine and her brother Edward.

But again in the same letter we have a passage that shows that her feet are still meshed in the net of Calvinistic theology. She writes: "My mind is often perplexed and such thoughts arise in it that I cannot pray, and I become bewildered. The wonder to me is, how all ministers and all Christians can feel themselves so inexcusably sinful, when it seems to me that we all come into the world in such a way that it would be miraculous if we did not sin! Mr. Hawes always says in his prayers, ' We have nothing to offer in extenuation of any of our sins,' and I always think when he says it that we have everything to offer in extenuation.

"The case seems to me exactly as if I had been brought into the world with such a thirst for ardent spirits that there was just a possibility, but no hope that I should resist, and then my eternal happiness made to depend on my being

temperate. Sometimes when I try to confess my sins I feel that I am more to be pitied than blamed, for I have never known the time when I have not had a temptation within me so strong that it was certain that I should not overcome it. This thought shocks me, but it comes with such force, and so appealingly, to all my consciousness, that it stifles all sense of sin."

It was such reflections and arguments as these that had aroused Doctor Beecher to despair over his daughter Catherine's spiritual condition. The fact was, he. belonged to one age and his children to another. Yet the brave old man lived to turnpathize with them.

Harriet at last learned to give up her introspection and morbid sensitiveness, and to live more healthily and humanly. At the age of twenty-one she was able to write thus to her friend Georgiana May: "After the disquisition on myself above cited you will be able to understand the wonderful changes through which *Ego et me ipse* has passed.

"The amount of the matter has been, as this inner world of mine has become worn out and untenable, I have at last concluded to come out of it and live in the eternal one, and, as F

S once advised me, give up the pernicious habit of meditation to the first Methodist minister who would take it, and try to mix in society somewhat as other persons would.

"' *Horas non numero non nisi serenas.*' Uncle Sam, who sits by me, has just been reading the above motto, the inscription on a sun-dial in Venice. It strikes me as having a distant relationship to what I was going to say. I have come to a firm resolution to count no hours but unclouded ones, and let all others slip out of my memory and reckoning as quickly as possible.

"I am trying to cultivate a spirit of general kindliness towards everybody. Instead of shrinking into a corner to notice how other people behave, I am holding out my hand to the right and to the left, and forming casual and incidental acquaintance with all who will be acquainted with me. In this way I find society full of interest and pleasure, — a pleasure that pleaseth me more because it is not old and worn out. From these friendships I expect little, and therefore generally receive more than I expect. From past friendships I have expected everything, and must of necessity have been disappointed. The kind words and looks that I call forth by looking and smiling are not much in themselves; but they form a very pretty flower-border to the way of life. They embellish the day or the hour as it passes, and when they fade they only do just as I expected they would. This kind of pleasure in acquaintance is new to me. I never tried it before. When I used to meet persons the first inquiry was, 'Have they such and such a character, or have they anything that might be of use or harm to me?'"

In this new life she was able to write to her brother Edward, "I have never been so happy as this summer. I began it in more suffering than I ever before have felt, but there is One whom I daily thank for all that suffering, since I hope that it has brought me at last to rest entirely in Him." So she learned to suffer and to love. To suffer and to love and at last to rest. After five years of struggling she returns to where she started when converted as a child of thirteen. Love became her gospel, the Alpha and Omega of her existence, love for her God, for her friends, and finally for humanity. The three words, "God is love," summed up her theology. Her love of humanity was not the vague charitable emotion which the phrase usually denotes. It was as real, as vital, and as impelling as the love for her friend which she thus expressed in closing this letter, —

"Oh, my dear G, it is scarcely well to love friends thus... those that I love; and oh, how much that word means. I feel sadly about them. They may change; they must die; they are separated from me, and I ask myself why should I wish to love with all the pains and penalties of such conditions? I check myself when expressing feelings like this, so much has been said of it by the sentimental, who talk what they could not have felt. But it is so deeply, sincerely so in me, that sometimes it will overflow. Well, there is a heaven — a heaven, — a world of love, and love after all is the life blood, the existence, the all in all of mind." CHAPTER in TEACHER AND WRITER

In January, 1831, Doctor Beecher, in the height of his Boston ministry in point of popularity and influence, began a series of sermons on the Roman Catholic Church, in which he sounded the alarm as to the supposed designs of the Papacy on the liberties of our nation. At this time he was considering a call to become president of the newly established Lane Theological Seminary at Walnut Hills, near Cincinnati, Ohio. The leading motive in determining him to accept this appointment was the desire to hold the great West for Protestantism. He was thrilled by the greatness of the enterprise. His whole family sympathized with him, and entered heartily into his plans. They felt that he was called to a great mission in which they all had a share. Catherine immediately determined to establish a school in Cincinnati to raise up teachers for the West.

In a letter to Miss May, Harriet, who was at this time about twenty years old, writes minutely and at length of their plans: "We mean to turn over the West by means of model schools in this its capital (Cincinnati). We mean to have a young ladies' school of about fifty or sixty, a primary school of little girls to the same amount, and then a primary school for boys. We have come to the conclusion that the work of teaching will never be rightly done till it comes into female hands.

"This is especially true with regard to boys. To govern boys by moral influence requires tact, and talent, and versatility; it requires also the same division of labor that female education does. But men of tact, versatility, talent, and piety, will not devote their lives to teaching. They must be ministers, and missionaries, and all that, and while there is such a thrilling call for action in this way, every man who is merely teaching feels as if he were a Hercules with a distaff ready to spring at the first trumpet that calls him away. As for division of labor, men must have salaries that can support wife and family, and, of course, a revenue would be required to support a requisite number of teachers if they could be found.

"Then, if men have more knowledge they have less talent in communicating it, nor have they the patience, the long-suffering, and the gentleness necessary to superintend the formation of character. We intend to make these principles understood, and ourselves to set the example of what females can do in this way. You see that first-rate talent is necessary for all that we mean to do, especially for the last, because here we must face down the prejudices of society, and we must have exemplary success to be believed. We want original planning minds, and you do not realize how few there are among females, and how few we can command of those that exist." Catherine had visited Cincinnati with her father before the removal was made, and had written to Harriet, "The folks are very anxious to have a school on our plan set on foot here. We can have fine rooms in the city college building, which is now unoccupied, and everybody is ready to lend a helping hand."

The sense of having a mission in the world was a ruling characteristic of the Beechers which Harriet shared to an unusual degree. It was only a strong sense of humor that saved them from fanaticism. Harriet took a very serious view of the migration of the family to the West, and believed most devoutly that it was in obedience to a divine call, and yet she could write thus from Philadelphia on the journey West: "I saw a notice in the *Philadelphian* about father, setting forth how 'this distinguished brother with his large family, having torn themselves from the endearing scenes of their home,' etc., 'were going like Jacob,' etc., — very scriptural and appropriate flourish. It is too much after the manner of men, as Paul says, 'speaking as a fool.'" This joyous, kindly humor is a strongly marked characteristic of the Beecher family. Mrs. Stowe often said that one of the most vivid impressions of her father's family as it was in her childhood was that of "a great household inspired by a spirit of cheerfulness and hilarity." Cheerfulness and hilarity is the characteristic Beecher atmosphere. The letter in which Mrs. Stowe pictures the events of the journey westward is overflowing with fun.

We have first a vivid picture of the sojourn in New York City; of Doctor Beecher rushing about in high spirits, soliciting funds for the new institution, preaching, dipping into books, and consulting authorities for his oration, "going around here, there, and everywhere; begging, borrowing, and spoiling the Egyptians, delighted with past success, and confident for the future." Harriet, however, finds New York too exciting and "scattering," and begins to long for "the waters of quietness."

They take the boat from New York and arrive in Philadelphia late on Saturday evening of a dull, drizzling day. Poor Aunt Esther Beecher and Mrs. Beecher are in despair over strayed trunks, for the recapture of which George Beecher, one of the sons, has been left behind. In the whole caravan not a clean dress or cap to put on! Part of the family are entertained at the house of Doctor Beecher's old friend, the Rev. Dr. Skinner, and Harriet with Catherine, Isabella, and James goes to the house of a Mrs. Elmes, — " rich, hospitable folks, who act the part of Gaius in apostolic times." The trunks arrive in a day or so, and Doctor Beecher, after seeing them safely landed in Doctor Skinner's entry, swings his hat around his head with a joyful, "Hurrah."

The next day they traveled about thirty miles in a private conveyance to Dowington. The driver was obliging, the roads good, and the scenery fine. All were in high spirits and gave vent to their joy in psalms and hymns. George had provided a goodly supply of tracts which they tossed to the wayfarers whom they met. Harriet declared that he was "peppering the land with moral and spir itual influences." As Harriet writes, they are comfortably seated in the front parlor of a little country inn, as much at home as if still in Boston. Doctor Beecher is reading. Thomas and Isabella are writing in their

daily journals. Catherine is writing to her sister, Mrs. Thomas Perkins, and Harriet to her friend, Georgiana May. She says, "Among the multitude of present friends my heart still makes occasional visits to absent ones, — visits full of cause for gratitude to Him who gives us friends. I have thought of you often today, my Georgiana. We stopped this noon at a substantial Pennsylvania tavern, and among the flowers in the garden was a late monthly honeysuckle, like the one in North Guilford. I made a spring for it; but George secured the finest bunch, which he wore in his button-hole the rest of the noon.

"This afternoon as we were traveling, we struck up and sang 'Jubilee.' It put me in mind of the time when we used to ride along the rough North Guilford roads, and make the air vocal as we went. Pleasant times, those! Those were blue skies, and that was a beautiful lake with pine trees that hung over it. But those we shall look upon 'na mair!'

"Well, my dear, there is a land where we shall not love and leave. Those skies shall never cease to shine, the waters of life we shall never be called upon to leave."

Sunday finds them in Harrisburg, sixty-two miles from Wheeling, where they were to take the boat for Cincinnati. On arriving in Wheeling the news of cholera in Cincinnati leads them to wait for eight days and then go on by private stage. Then, again, at Granville they spend part of a week and assist at revival meetings.

Arrived at Walnut Hills, Harriet, in the first blush of her enthusiasm, writes to Georgiana May this glowing description of the new home: "How I wish you could see Walnut Hills! It is about two miles from the city, and the road to it is as picturesque as you can imagine a road to be, without 'springs that run among the hills.' Every possible variety of hill and vale of beautiful slope, and undulations of land set off by velvet richness of turf, and broken up by groves and forests of every outline of foliage, make the scene Arcadian. You might ride over the same road a dozen times a day, untired, for the constant

variation of view caused by ascending and descending hill relieves you from all tedium. Much of the wooding is beech of a noble growth. The straight, beautiful shafts of these trees as one looks up the cool green recesses of the woods seem as though they might form very proper columns for a Dryad temple."

Miss Catherine Beecher thus pictures the site of the seminary: "The Seminary is located on a farm of one hundred and twenty-five acres of fine land, with groves of superb trees around it.... I have become somewhat acquainted with those ladies we shall have the most to do with, and find them intelligent New England sort of folks. Indeed, Cincinnati is a New England city in all its habits, and its inhabitants are more than half from New England.

"The second church, which is the best in the city, will give father a unanimous call to be their minister, with the understanding that he will give them what time he can spare from the Seminary."

Many years afterwards Mrs. Stowe, writing of her life in Cincinnati at this time, says: "Doctor Beecher's house on Walnut Hills was in many respects peculiarly pleasant. It was a two-story brick edifice of moderate dimensions, fronting the West with a long L running back into the primeval forest, or grove, as it was familiarly called, which here came up to the very door. Immense trees, beech, black oak, and others, spread their protecting arms over the back yard, affording in summer an almost impenetrable shade.

"An airy veranda was built in the angle formed by the L along the entire inner surface of the house, from which during the fierce gales of autumn and winter we used to watch the tossing of the spectral branches and listen to the roaring of wind through the forest."

"... During the first year of Doctor Beecher's Walnut Hills life the care of the family was shared by Mrs. Beecher and Aunt Esther, though, as the health of the former declined, the burden fell more and more upon the latter. The family was large, comprising, including servants, thirteen in all, besides occasional visitors.

"The house was full. There was a continual high tide of life and animation. The old carryall was continually vibrating between home and the city, and the excitement of going and coming rendered anything like stagnation an impossibility.... It was an exuberant and glorious life while it lasted. The atmosphere of his household was replete with moral oxygen, — full charged with intellectual electricity. Nowhere else have I felt anything resembling or equaling it. It was a kind of moral heaven, the purity, vivacity, and inspiration of which only those can appreciate who have felt it."

In 1832 while visiting her brother William in Newport, Rhode Island, Harriet had begun an elementary geography. This little book, her first published work, was completed during the winter of 1833, and published by Corey, Fairbank & Webster of Cincinnati. Shortly after its publication she writes to Miss May, " Bishop Purcell visited our school to-day, and expressed himself as greatly pleased that we had opened such an one here. He spoke of my poor little geography and thanked me for the unprejudiced manner in which I had handled the Catholic question in it. I was of course flattered that he should have known anything about the book."

When we remember that Doctor Beecher's great motive in going to Cincinnati was to oppose the influence of the Roman Catholic Church in every way possible, and that he frequently attacked it in the pulpit and in the press, this incident reflects great credit, not only on the wisdom and tolerance of Archbishop Purcell, but on that of Harriet Beecher as well. When the father, whom the daughter revered, honestly regarded the Catholic Church as a great evil, and a peril to our free institutions, it required no little courage and independence of thought in the daughter to so handle the Catholic question as to win words of hearty appreciation from one of the highest ecclesiastics of that communion. That the good bishop visited the school and made such kind comments on its mission showed a broad, wise, and tolerant spirit which must have tended to confirm in Harriet's mind what she had often heard her uncle Samuel say in the old Litchfield days about the Roman Catholic prelates, whom he carried on his ships between Spain and America, being as learned and as devoted to the good of men as any Protestants to be found in America.

With all her enthusiasm and ideality, Harriet nevertheless felt the wear and tear of the routine work of the schoolroom. She writes to Miss May during the first year of her school life in Cincinnati: "Since writing the above my whole time has been taken up in the labor of our new school, or wasted in the fatigue and lassitude following such labor....

"Now, Georgiana, let me copy for your delectation a list of matters that I have jotted down for consideration at a teachers' meeting to be held to-morrow night. It runneth as follows. Just hear!' About quills and paper on the floor; forming classes; drinking in the entry (cold water, mind you); giving leave to speak; recess bell,' etc.,' You are tired, I see,' said John Gilpin, so am I! and I spare you.

"I have just been hearing a class of little girls recite, and telling them a fairy story that I had to spin out as it went along beginning with, 'Once upon a time there was,' etc., in the good old-fashioned way of stories."

To conceive great things is to smoke enchanted cigarettes, but to execute is drudgery. Harriet learned to know such drudgery in full measure. Her ill-health was largely due to unregulated and unrestrained feeling. She lived overmuch in her emotions. Nothing like drudgery to tame the feelings! About this time she writes to Miss May, " To-day is Sunday, and I am staying at home because I think it is time to take some efficient means to dissipate the illness and bad feelings of various kinds that have for some time been growing upon me. At present there is and can be very little system and regularity about me. About half of my time I am scarcely alive, and a great part of the rest, the slave and sport of morbid feeling and unreasonable prejudice. I have everything but good health.... How good it would be for me to be put in a place that breaks up and precludes thought. Thought, intense, emotional thought, has been my disease. How much good it would do me to be where I could not but be thoughtless....

"Recently I have been reading the life of Madame de Stael and 'Corinne,' I have felt an intense sympathy with many parts of that book, with many parts of her character. But in America feelings vehement and absorbing like hers become still more deep, morbid, and impassioned by the constant habits of self-government which the rigid forms of our society demand. They are repressed and they burn inwardly till they burn the very soul, leaving only dust and ashes. It seems to me that the intensity with which my mind has thought and felt on every subject presented to it has had this effect. It has withered and exhausted it, and though young I have no sympathy with the feelings of youth. All that is enthusiastic, all that is impassioned in admiration of nature, of writing, of character, in devotional thought and emotion, or in emotions of affection, I have felt with vehement and absorbing intensity, — felt till my mind is exhausted and seems to be sinking into deadness. Half of my time I am glad to remain in a listless vacancy; to busy myself with trifles since thought is pain and emotion is pain." The sense of humor was for Mrs. Stowe indeed a saving grace. She could not have lived without it. Her nature so intense and emotional would, to use her own figure, have burned itself to ashes. Her letters at this time are full of playfulness. For example, she writes to her sister Mrs. Perkins in Hartford: "By the by, Mary, speaking of the temptations of cities, I have much solicitude on Jamie's account lest he should form improper intimacies, for yesterday or the day before we saw him parading by the house with his arm over the neck of a great hog, apparently on the most intimate terms possible; the other day he actually got on the back of one and rode some distance. So much for allowing these animals to promenade the streets, a particular in which Mrs. Cincinnati has imitated the domestic arrangement of some of her elder sisters, and a very disgusting one it is!" Of the same quiet vein of humor is the description of the family physician. "Our family physician is one Dr. Drake, a man of a good deal of science, theory, and reputed skill, but a sort of general mark for the opposition of all the medical cloth of the city. He is a tall, rectangular, perpendicular sort of a body, stiff as a poker, and enunciates his prescriptions much as if he were giving a discourse on the doctrine of election. The other evening he was detained from visiting Kate, and sent a very polite, ceremonious note containing a prescription, with Dr. D.'s compliments to Miss Beecher, requesting that she would take the inclosed with a little molasses at nine o'clock precisely." These descriptions of the life about her would hardly seem to come from the young woman who had written, "About half my time I am scarcely alive."

It was during her first year in Cincinnati that Harriet, in company with a Miss Dutton, one of the teachers in the school, made a visit to a Kentucky slave plantation. Years afterward, on reading "Uncle Tom's Cabin," Miss Dutton commented with amazement that, although during this visit Harriet had seemed too dreamy and abstracted to notice what was passing about her, nevertheless scenes, incidents, and persons, met with during this brief visit, were graphically reproduced and woven into the texture of her story.

About this time a wealthy and cultivated family came from Louisiana to Ohio, and settled near Cincinnati. They brought with them a number of slaves whom they set at liberty, and among them was a quaint little Jim Crow of a negro girl who was the original of "Topsy." It was in attempting to give this wild little savage some religious instruction, in a little mission Sunday-school, that Mrs. Stowe got her material for the celebrated dialogue between Miss Ophelia and Topsy.

"Miss Ophelia, 'Have you ever heard anything about God, Topsy?'

"The child looked bewildered but grinned as usual.

"' Do you know who made you?'

"' Nobody as I knows on,' said the child with a short laugh.

"The idea appeared to amuse her considerably; for her eyes twinkled, and she added: —

"' I 'spect I grow'd, nobody never made me!'"

Harriet's two uncles, Captain Samuel Foote and Mr. John Foote, also lived in Cincinnati at this time. Captain Samuel Foote's house was on a height in the upper part of the city, and commanded a fine view of the whole lower town. It was a centre for persons of artistic and literary tastes. Here often met the "Semi-Colon Club," among the membership of which were names afterwards as prominent in state and national affairs as those of Salmon P. Chase; Mrs. Peters, founder of the Philadelphia School of Design; Mrs. Caroline Lee Hentz; C. P. Cranch, the poet; Worthington Whittredge, the artist; General Edward King, Miss Catherine Beecher, Professor Calvin E. Stowe, Judge James Hall, editor of the *Western Magazine,* and many others.

At the meetings of this club the members read papers and stories, or discussed interesting topics previously announced. In a letter to Miss May, Harriet Beecher gives an amusing description of her part in these meetings: "I am wondering as to what I shall do next. I have been writing a piece to be read next Monday evening at Uncle Sam's soiree (the Semi-Colon). It is a letter purporting to be from Dr. Johnson. I have been stilting about in his style so long that it is a relief to me to come down to the jog of common English. Now, I think of it, I will just give you a history of my campaign in this circle.

"My first piece was a letter from Bishop Butler, written in his outrageous style of parenthesis and fogification. My second, a satirical essay on the modern uses of languages. This I shall send to you as some of the gentlemen, it seems, took a fancy to it, and requested leave to put it in the *Western Magazine.*

It is ascribed to Catherine, or I don't know that I should let it go. I have no notion of appearing in *propria persona.* "The next piece was a satire on certain members who were getting very much into the way of joking on the worn-out subjects of matrimony and old maid and old bachelorism. I therefore wrote a set of legislative enactments purporting to be from the ladies of the society forbidding all such allusions in the future. It made some sport at the time. I try not to be personal, and to be courteous even in satire.

"But I have written a piece this week that is making me some disquiet. I did not like it that there was so little that was serious and rational about the reading. So I conceived the design of writing a set of letters and throwing them in as being the letters of a friend.

"I wrote a letter this week for the first of the set, — easy, not very sprightly, — describing an imaginary situation, a house in the country, a gentleman and lady, Mr. and Mrs. Howard, as being pious, literary, and agreeable. I threw into the letter a number of little particulars and incidental allusions to give it the air of having been really a letter. I meant thus to give myself an opportunity for the introduction of different subjects and the discussion of different characters in future letters.

"I meant to write on a great number of projects in the future. Cousin Elizabeth only was in the secret; Uncle Samuel and Sarah Eliot were not to know.

"Yesterday morning I finished my letter, smoked it to make it look yellow, tore it to make it look old, directed it and scratched out the direction, postmarked it with red ink, sealed it and broke the seal, all this to give credibility to the fact of its being a real letter. Then I inclosed it in an envelope, stating that it was a part of a set that had fallen into my hands. This envelope was written in a scrawny, scrawly gentleman's hand.

"I put it into the office in the morning, directed it to 'Mrs. Samuel E. Foote,' and then sent word to Sis that it was coming, so that she might be ready to enact the part.

"Well, the deception took. Uncle Sam

examined it and pronounced, *ex cathedra,* that it must have been a real letter. Mr. Greene (the gentleman who reads) declared that it must have come from Mrs. Hall, and elucidated the theory by spelling out the names and dates that I had had erased, which, of course, he accommodated to his own tastes. But then, what makes me feel uneasy is that Elizabeth, after reading it, did not seem to be exactly satisfied. She thought it had too much sentiment, too much particularity of incident, — she did not exactly know what. She was afraid it would be criticised unmercifully. Now, Elizabeth has a tact and quickness of perception that I trust to, and her remarks have made me uneasy enough. I am unused to being criticised, and don't know how I shall bear it."

It was about this time that Judge Hall offered a prize of fifty dollars for the best short story that should be sent in to the *Western Magazine* within a given period. The prize was awarded to Harriet Beecher for a story entitled "Uncle Lot," which was afterwards incorporated in the "Mayflower," published by Harper & Brothers in 1843. It was at this time that Harriet Beecher was laying the foundation of her fame as a writer. In a letter to Mrs. Follen, written immediately after the publication of "Uncle Tom's Cabin," she gives the following account of the way she came to be a writer: "During long years of struggling with poverty and sickness, and a hot, debilitating climate, my children grew up around me. The nursery and the kitchen were my principal fields of labor. Some of my friends, pitying my trials, copied and sent a number of little sketches from my pen to a number of liberally paying Annuals, with my name. With the first money that I earned in this way I bought a featherbed! For as I had married into poverty and without a dowry, and as my husband had only a large library of books and a great deal of learning, the bed and pillows were thought the most profitable investment.

"After this I thought I had discovered the philosopher's stone. So when a new carpet or mattress was going to be needed, or when at the close of the year it

began to be evident that my family accounts, like poor Dora's, 'would n't add up,' then I used to say to my faithful friend and factotum Anna, who shared all my joys and sorrows, 'Now, if you will keep the babies, and attend to the things in the house for one day, I 'll write a piece, and then we shall be out of the scrape.'

"So I became an author, — very modest at first, I do assure you, and remonstrating very seriously with friends who had thought it best to put my name to the pieces by way of getting up a reputation; and if you see a wood-cut of me, with an immoderately long nose, on the cover of all the U. S. Almanacs, I wish you to take notice that I have been forced into it contrary to my natural modesty by the imperative solicitations of my dear five thousand friends, and the public generally."

So it appears that writing was with Mrs. Stowe before marriage a diversion, but after marriage a stern necessity.

Miss Catherine Beecher wrote this graphic account of her efforts in stirring her sister up to literary activity after her marriage: "During a visit to her Mrs. Stowe, I had an opportunity one day of witnessing the combined exercise of her literary and domestic genius in a style that to me was quite amusing.

"'Come, Harriet,' said I, as I found her tending one baby and watching two others just able to walk, 'where is that piece for the *Souvenir* which I promised the editor I would get from you and send him on next week? You have only this one day left to finish it, and have it I must.'

"'And how will you get it, sister of mine?' said Harriet. 'You will have at least to wait till I get house-cleaning over and baby's teeth through.'

"'As to house-cleaning, you can defer it one day longer; and as to baby's teeth there is no end to them as I can see. No, to-day that story must be ended. There Frederick has been sitting by Ellen and saying all those pretty things for more than a month now, and she has been turning and blushing till I am sure it is time to go to her relief.

"' Come, it would not take you three

hours at the rate you can write to finish the courtship, marriage, catastrophe, *eclaircissement* and all; and this three hours of your brains will earn enough to pay for all the sewing your fingers could do for a year to come. Two dollars a page, my dear, and you can write a page in fifteen minutes! Come, then, my lady housekeeper, economy is a cardinal virtue; consider the economy of the thing.'

"' But, my dear, here is a baby in my arms, and two little pussies by my side, and there is a great baking down in the kitchen, and there is a green girl for help, besides preparations to be made for house-cleaning next week. It is really out of the question, you see.'

"' I see no such thing. I do not know what genius is given for if it is not to help a woman out of a scrape. Come set your wits to work and let me have my way, and you shall have all the work done, and finish the story too.'

"'Well, but kitchen affairs?'

"' We can manage them too. You know that you can write anywhere, and anyhow. Just take your seat at the kitchen table with your writing weapons, and while you superintend Mina, fill up the odd snatches of time with the labors of your pen.'

"I carried my point. In ten minutes she was seated; a table with flour, rolling-pin, ginger, and lard on one side; a dresser with eggs, pork, and beans and various cooking utensils on the other, near her an oven heating, and beside her a darkskinned nymph waiting for orders.

"' Here, Harriet,' said I, 'you can write on this atlas in your lap; no matter how the writing looks, I will copy it.'

"' Well, well,' she said, with a resigned sort of an amused look. 'Mina, you may do what I told you, while I write a few minutes, till it is time to mould up the bread. Where is the inkstand?'

"' Here it is, on top of the tea-kettle, close by,' said I.

"At this Mina giggled, and we both laughed to see her merriment at our literary proceedings.

"I began to overhaul the portfolio to

find the right sheet. 'Here it is,' said I,' here is Frederick sitting by Ellen glancing at her brilliant face, and saying something about "guardian angel," and all that — you remember?'

"'Yes, yes,' she said, falling into a muse as she attempted to recover the thread of her story.

"' Ma'am, shall I put the pork on the top of the beans?' asked Mina.

"' Come, come,' said Harriet, laughing. 'You see how it is. Mina is a new hand and cannot do anything without me to direct her. We must give up the writing for to-day.'

"' No, no, let us have another trial. You can dictate as easily as you can write. Come, I can set the baby in this clothes basket and give him some mischief or another to keep him quiet; you shall dictate and I will write. Now, this is the place where you left off: you were describing the scene between Ellen and her lover: the last sentence was, " Borne down by the tide of agony she leaned her head on her hands, the tears streamed through her fingers, and her whole frame shook with convulsive sobs." What next?'

"' Mina, pour a little milk into this pearlash!' said Harriet.

"'Come,' said I, '"The tears streamed through her fingers, and her whole frame shook with convulsive sobs." What next?'

"Harriet paused, and looked musingly out of the window as she turned her mind to her story. 'You may write now,' said she, and she dictated as follows: —

"' Her lover wept with her, nor dared again to touch the point so sacredly guarded. —Mina, roll that crust a little thinner.—He spoke in soothing tones.

"' — Mina poke the coals in the oven.

"' Here,' said I,' let me direct Mina about these matters and write a while yourself.'

"Harriet took the pen and patiently set herself to work. For a while my culinary knowledge and skill were proof to all Mina's investigating inquiries, and they did not fail till I saw two pages completed.

"'You have done bravely,' said I, as

I read over the manuscript;'now you must direct Mina a while. Meantime dictate, and I will write.'

"Never was there a more docile literary lady than my sister. Without a word of objection she followed my request.

"'lam ready to write,' said I. 'The last sentence was, "What is this life to one who has suffered as I have?" What next?'

"' Shall I put in the brown, or the white bread first?' asked Mina.

"' The brown first,' said Harriet.

"' " What is this life to one who has suffered as I have?"'said I.

"Harriet brushed the flour off her apron, and sat down for a moment in a muse. Then she dictated as follows: —

"' Under the breaking of my heart I have borne up. I have borne up under all that tries a woman, —but this thought,—oh, Henry!'

"'Ma'am, shall I put ginger in this pumpkin?/ queried Mina.

"' No, you may let that alone just now,' replied Harriet. She then proceeded:—

"' I know my duty to my children. I see the hour must come. You must take them, Henry; they are my last earthly comfort.'

"' Ma'am, what shall I do with these egg-shells, and all this truck here?' interrupted Mina.

"' Put them in the pail by you,' answered Harriet.

"'" They are my last earthly comfort,"' said I. 'What next?'

"She continued to dictate, —

"'You must take them away. It may be — perhaps it must be — that I shall soon follow, but the breaking heart of a wife still pleads, "a little longer, a little longer."'

"'How much longer must the gingerbread stay in?' asked Mina.

"' five minutes,' said Harriet.

"'" A little longer, a little longer,"' I repeated in a dolorous tone, and we burst out into a laugh.

"Thus we went on, cooking, writing, nursing, and laughing, till I finally accomplished my object. The piece was finished and copied, and the next day sent to the editor."

No wonder Mrs. Stowe describes her writing as "rowing against wind and tide!"

During the summer of 1834 the young writer made her first visit to New England since leaving there for the West two years before. The occasion was the graduation of her brother, Henry Ward, from Amherst College. She covered the earlier part of the trip by stage to Toledo, and thence by steamer to Buffalo. It was on this journey that she saw Niagara for the first time, and in a letter to Mrs. Samuel Foote she thus pictures her sensations: "I did not once think whether it was high or low; whether it roared or did n't roar; whether it equaled my expectations or not. My mind whirled off it seemed to me into a new and strange world. It seemed unearthly, like the strange dim images in the book of Revelation.

"I thought of the great white throne; the rainbow around it; the throne in sight like unto an emerald; and 0, that beautiful water rising like moonlight, falling as the soul sinks when it dies, to rise refined, spiritualized, and pure. That rainbow breaking out, trembling, fading, and again coming like a beautiful spirit walking the waters.

"Oh, it is lovelier than it is great; it is like the mind that made it, great, but so veiled in beauty that we gaze without terror. I felt as if I could have gone over with the waters; it would be so beautiful a death; there would be no fear in it.

"I felt the very rock tremble under me with a sort of joy. I was so maddened that I could have gone, too, if it had gone." CHAPTER IV WIFE AND MOTHER

Harriet Beecher's journey to the East was saddened by the news of the death of her intimate friend, Mrs. Stowe, wife of Professor Calvin Ellis Stowe. Mrs. Stowe was a daughter of the Rev. Bennet Tyler, at one time the president of Dartmouth College, then Doctor Payson's successor in Portland, Maine, and finally president of East Windsor Theological Seminary, in Connecticut. She was beautiful, talented, and had a wonderful voice, and all this, added to unusual dignity and sweetness of character, had made her universally loved.

In a letter written to her sister Mary, Harriet had thus described Mrs. Stowe: "Let me introduce you to Mrs. Stowe, — a delicate, pretty little woman, with hazel eyes, auburn hair, fair complexion, fine color, a pretty little mouth, fine teeth, and a most interesting timidity and simplicity of manner; I fell in love with her directly."

His loss drove Professor Stowe nearly insane, and Harriet on her return to Cincinnati became his comforter. In about two years this friendship ripened into love, and they became engaged. Harriet seized the last moments before the wedding to write to Miss May.

Cincinnati, *Jan.* 6,1836. Well, my dear G., about half an hour more, and your old friend, companion, schoolmate, sister, etc., will cease to be Hattie Beecher and change to nobody knows who. My dear, you are engaged, and pledged in a year or two to encounter a similar fate, and do you wish to know how you will feel? Well, my dear, I have been dreading the time, and lying awake all last week wondering how I should live through this overwhelming crisis, and lo! it has come and I feel nothing at all. The wedding is to be altogether domestic, nobody present but my own brothers and sisters, and my old colleague, Mary Dutton; and as there is a sufficiency of the ministry we have not even to call in the foreign aid of a minister. Sister Katy is not here, so she will not witness my departure from her care and guidance to that of another. None of my numerous friends and acquaintances who have taken such a deep interest in making the connection for me even know the day, and it will all be done and over before they know anything about it.

Well, it is a mercy to have this entire apathy come over one at this time. I should be crazy to feel as I did yesterday, or indeed to feel anything at all. But I inwardly vowed that my last feelings and reflections on this subject should be yours, and as I have not got any it is just as well to tell you that. Well, here comes Mr. Stowe, so farewell, and so for the last time I subscribe myself

Your own

Hattie E. Beecher.

The letter was not posted, and she later added: "Three weeks have passed since writing the above, and my husband and I are now seated by our own fireside, as domestic as any pair of tame fowl you ever saw; he writing to his mother, and I to you.

"Two days after our marriage we took a wedding excursion so called, though we would have most gladly been excused this conformity to ordinary custom, had not necessity required Mr. Stowe to visit Columbus, and I had too much divisiveness not to go too. Ohio roads at this season are no joke, I can tell you, though we were, on the whole, wonderfully taken care of, and our expedition included as many pleasures as an expedition at this time of the year ever could.

"And now, my dear, perhaps the wonder to you, as to me, is, how this momentous crisis in the life of such a whisp of nerve as myself has been transacted so quietly. My dear, it is a wonder to myself. I am tranquil, quiet, and happy. I look only on the present and leave the future to Him who has hitherto been so kind to me.

"' Take no thought for the morrow' is my motto, and my comfort is to rest on Him in whose house there are many mansions provided when these fleeting earthly ones shall pass away."

Largely through the influence of his very warm friend, General Harrison, Professor Stowe had been appointed a commissioner by the State of Ohio to investigate and report on the public school systems of Europe. To this commission was soon added another. The faculty and friends of Lane Seminary found this an excellent opportunity to make many sorely needed additions to the seminary library, and intrusted him with funds for the purpose. Professor Stowe, since his arrival in Ohio, had been untiring in his labors for popular education. It was largely through his influence that "The College of Teachers" was founded in Cincinnati in 1833, the object of which was to popularize the common schools by increasing their

teaching efficiency, and so to increase the demand for education among the people. He was ably seconded in his efforts by such prominent citizens as General Harrison, Smith *Grixak6,* Archbishop Purcell, A. H. McGuffey, Doctor Beecher, Lydia Sigourney, and others. Mr. Stowe sailed from New York on the ship Montreal, June 8, 1836, just five months after his marriage.

During her husband's absence Mrs. Stowe continued to live at her father's house, and employed herself in writing short stories, articles, and essays which appeared from time to time in the *Western Monthly Magazine,* the *New York Evangelist,* and other publications. She also assisted her brother Henry Ward in editing the *Journal,* a small daily paper published in Cincinnati. In the letter to Mrs. Follen, already referred to, she gives this account of her early married life: "I was married when I was twenty-five years of age to a man rich in Greek and Hebrew, Latin and Arabic, and, alas, rich in nothing else. When I went to housekeeping, my entire stock of China for parlor and kitchen was bought for eleven dollars. That lasted very well for two years till my brother was married, and brought his bride to visit us. I then found, on review, that I had neither plates nor teacups to set a table for my father's family; whereupon I thought it best to reinforce the establishment by getting me a teaset that cost ten dollars more, and this, I believe, formed my whole stock in trade for many years.

"But then I was abundantly enriched with wealth of another sort. I had two little, curlyheaded twin daughters to begin with, and my stock in this line has gradually increased till I have been the mother of seven children, the most beautiful and the most loved of whom lies buried near my Cincinnati residence.

"I lived two miles from the city of Cincinnati, in the country, and domestic service, not always to be found you know in the city, is next to an impossibility to obtain in the country, even by those who are willing to give the highest wages; so what was to be expected for poor me, who had very little of this world's goods to offer?

"Had it not been for my inseparable friend, Anna, a noble-hearted English girl, who landed on our shores in destitution and sorrow, and clave to me as Ruth to Naomi, I had never lived through all the trials which this uncertainty and want of domestic service imposed upon us both."

While Professor Stowe was abroad his wife kept him informed of the very significant events that took place in Cincinnati during the summer and fall of the year 1836. The burning question of negro slavery had begun to be agitated in Cincinnati, and Lane Theological Seminary came to be looked upon as a hot-bed of abolitionism.

The Abolition movement was confined to the students, however, and was led by Mr. Theodore D. Weld, a man of remarkable decision and energy of character. He was unusually eloquent, a strong, logical reasoner, and his personal influence was even greater than his eloquence, though that enabled him to hold crowded audiences spellbound for many hours together. He had earned money for his education by lecturing through the Southern States, and what he then saw of slavery made him, from the depths of his soul, its bitter enemy. He had succeeded in converting a number of slave-holders to his views. Among them was Mr. James G. Birney, of Huntsville, Alabama, who not only liberated his own slaves, but in connection with Dr. Gamaliel Bailey of Cincinnati, founded and conducted in that city an Abolition paper called the *Philanthropist*. This was the paper which was suppressed, and its office wrecked by a mob, as recounted in Mrs. Stowe's letter which follows: "Yesterday evening I spent scribbling for Henry's newspaper, the *Journal*. It was in this wise: 'Birney's printing press has been mobbed, and many of the respectable citizens are inclined to wink at the outrage in consideration of its moving in the line of their prejudices.'

"I wrote a conversational sketch, in which I rather satirized this inconsistent spirit, and brought out the evil results of patronizing any violation of private rights. It was in a light, sketchy vein, and designed to draw attention to a long editorial of Henry's in which he considered the subject fully and seriously. His piece is, I think, a powerful one; indeed, he does write very strongly. I am quite proud of his editorials; they are well studied, earnest, and dignified. I think he will make a first-rate writer. Both of our pieces have gone to press to-day, with Charles' article on music, and we have had not a little diversion about our family newspaper.

"I thought when I was writing last night, that I was like a good wife defending one of your principles in your absence, and wanted you to see how manfully I talked about it. Henry has also taken up and examined the question of the Seminole Indians and done it very nobly.

"The excitement about Birney continues to increase. The keeper of the Franklin Hotel was assailed by a document subscribed to by many of his boarders demanding that Birney should be turned out of doors. He chose to negative the demand, and twelve of his boarders immediately left.... A meeting has been convoked by means of a hand-bill, in which some of the most respectable men of the city are invited by name to come together and consider whether they will allow Mr. Birney to continue his paper in the city. Mr. Greene says that, to his utter surprise, many of the most respectable and influential citizens gave out that they should go.

"He was one of the number they invited, but he told those who came to him that he would have nothing to do with disorderly public meetings, or mobs in any shape, and that he was entirely opposed to the whole thing.

"I presume they will have a hot meeting if they have any at all. I wish father were at home to preach a sermon to his church, for many of the members do not frown on these things as they ought.

"Later: The meeting was held.... The mob madness is certainly upon this city when men of sense and standing will pass resolutions approving in so many words of things done contrary to law, as one of the resolutions of this meeting did. It quoted the demolition of the tea in Boston harbor as being authority and precedent.

"A large body, perhaps the majority, of citizens disapprove, but I fear there will not be public disavowal.... The editor of the *Gazette,* in a very dignified and judicious manner, has condemned the whole thing, and Henry has opposed, but otherwise the papers have either been silent or in favor of the mobs. We shall see what the result will be in a few days.

"For my part I can easily see how such proceedings may make converts to abolitionism, for already my sympathies are strongly enlisted for Mr. Birney, and I hope he will stand his ground and assert his rights.

"The office is fire-proof and inclosed by high walls. I wish he would man it with armed men and see what can be done. If I were a man, I would go for one, and take good care of at least one window. Henry sits opposite to me writing a most valiant editorial, and tells me to tell you he is waxing mighty in battle."

One day during this period Mrs. Stowe found Henry in the kitchen busily engaged in making lead bullets for his pistols.

"What are you making those for, Henry?" she asked.

"To kill men with, Hattie!" he replied. Many years later in telling this incident to her son, Mrs. Stowe said, "I never saw Henry look so terrible! I did not like it, for I feared he was growing blood-thirsty."

"Were you never afraid, mother?" asked her son.

"No, I don't remember being afraid exactly,— I was excited, indignant, and thoroughly roused."

"I suppose that there was danger both then and afterwards," she added, "but we were protected by the distance of Lane Seminary from the city, and the Providential depth and adhesiveness of the Cincinnati mud in those days."

In her next letter to her husband, she says: "I told you in my last that the mob broke into Birney's press, where, however, the mischief done was but slight. The object appeared to be principally to terrify. Immediately there followed a general excitement in which even good men in their panic and prejudice about abolitionism forgot that mobs were worse evils than that, talked against Birney, and winked at the outrage.... Meanwhile, the turbulent spirits went beyond this and talked of revolution and of righting things without law that could not be righted by it..., A meeting was convoked at lower Market St. to decide whether they would tolerate the publication of an Abolition paper, and to this meeting all the most respectable citizens were by name summoned.

"There were four classes in the city then: Those who meant to go as revolutionists, and support the mob; those who meant to put down Birney but rather hoped to do it without a mob; those who felt ashamed to go, foreseeing the probable consequences, and yet did not decidedly frown upon it; those who sternly and decidedly reprehended it."

In the next paragraph we learn that Salmon P. Chase was prominent in this last class.

She continues: "All the papers in the city with the exception of Hammond's and Henry's were either silent or openly mobocratic. As might have been expected, Birney refused to leave, and that night the mob tore down his press, scattered the types, dragged the whole to the river and threw it in, and then came back to demolish the office.

"... The mayor was a silent spectator of these proceedings, and was heard to say, 'Well, lads, you have done well, so far; go home now before you disgrace yourselves'; but the 'lads' spent the rest of the night, and a greater part of the next day, Sunday, in pulling down the houses of inoffensive and respectable blacks. The *Gazette* office was threatened, the *Journal* office was to go next; Lane Seminary and the water works were also mentioned as probable points to be attacked by the mob.

"By Tuesday morning the city was pretty well alarmed. A regular corps of volunteers was organized, who for three nights patrolled the streets with firearms, and with legal warrant from the mayor, who by this time was glad to give it, to put down the mob even by bloodshed.

"For a day or two we did not know but there would actually be war to the knife, as was threatened by the mob, and we really saw Henry depart with his pistols with daily alarm, only we were all too full of patriotism not to have sent every brother we had rather than not have had the principles of freedom and order defended.

"But here the tide turned. The mob, unsupported by a now frightened community, slunk into their dens, and were still,..."

In speaking of the events of this crucial time in her life Mrs. Stowe once said to her son: "I saw for the first time clearly that the institution of slavery was incapable of defence, and that it was for that reason that its supporters were compelled to resort to mob-violence. I saw that it was clearly incompatible with our free institutions and was confident that it was doomed, and that it would go, but how or when I could not picture to myself. That summer and fall opened my eyes to the real nature of slavery as they had never been opened before."

In September, 1836, while her husband was still in Europe, Mrs. Stowe gave birth to twin daughters, Eliza and Isabella as she named them, but when Professor Stowe landed in New York in January, 1837, after a two months' passage by sailing ship, he insisted that they should be called Eliza Tyler and Harriet Beecher.

In the summer of 1837 Mrs. Stowe's health forced her to put aside household cares, and accordingly she made a long visit at the house of her brother, the Rev. William Beecher, in Putnam, Ohio. From Putnam she writes: "The good people here, you know, are about half Abolitionists. A lady who takes a leading part in the female society in this place, called yesterday and brought Catherine the proceedings of the Female Anti-Slavery Convention.

"I should think them about as ultra as to measures as anything that has been attempted, though I am glad to see a better spirit than marks such proceedings generally.

"To-day I read some in Mr. Birney's *Philanthropist.* Abolition being the fashion here it is natural to look at its papers. It does seem to me there needs to be an intermediate society. If not, as light increases, all the excesses of the Abolition party will not prevent humane and conscientious men from joining it."

The attitude of Mrs. Stowe and her husband at this time towards the Abolition party was very similar to the position of thousands of thoughtful people to-day with regard to the Socialist party. While deploring its excesses and unwisdom in many particulars, they know it stands for great and radical reforms for which there is a crying need.

At the close of the letter Mrs. Stowe adds: "Pray what is there in Cincinnati to satisfy one whose mind is awakened on this subject (slavery)? No one can have the system of slavery brought before him without an irrepressible desire to do something, and what is there to be done?"

Little did she then dream that she was "to do something " which would be as potent as any other one thing in "cutting the Gordian knot" of this giant problem. At this time her husband wrote her, "We all of course feel proper indignation at the doings of the last General Assembly, and shall treat them with merited contempt. This alliance between the Old School Presbyterians and the slaveholders will make more Abolitionists than anything that has been done yet."

Great events hung like storm clouds on the horizon of the year 1838. In May of that year the powerful Presbyterian Church of the United States was rent asunder, the nominal cause being differences in theological opinion, the underlying cause slavery. Doctor Beecher and his sons were conspicuous leaders in this great secession. At this time a Lane student writes to Mrs. Stowe from Philadelphia as follows: "Your father and brother distinguished themselves in the Convention on Monday and Tuesday. I did not hear them —did not reach

Philadelphia till yesterday evening.

"The Assembly is by no means the most exciting matter at present to the citizens. The heavens at this moment are lighted up by the flames of the Abolition or Liberty Hall in Sixth Street. The mob have set it on fire. It was dedicated two weeks ago, and cost forty thousand dollars. The AntiSlavery Society are holding a convention in it. Miss Grimke'jOr rather Mrs. Weld,1 spoke there (she was married on Tuesday). The mob broke the windows. Dr. Parrish told them not to hold nigrht-meetings; but they would. The ladies walk arm in arm with the blacks. I was there this afternoon: the women were holding a convention. The streets were thronged by the mob watching the door.

"So long as the Abolitionists kept away from the negroes the street was still as the grave, —the mob only looked on, — but when they saw a huge negro darken the door with a fair Quaker girl hanging on his arm, they screamed and swore vengeance. The Mayor and Sheriff were on the ground. The fire raged with great violence. The fire engines refused to play upon the building.... The bell of the State House is tolling again — there are cries of fire!... The heavens are lighted up! The African Hall on Thirteenth St. is on fire. The mob is cutting the hose that no water may reach it.... That the Convention have been imprudent there is no doubt; but that the rabble in the midst of a powerful and enlightened community should be permitted to trample on all law is shameful." 1 The wife of Theodore D. Weld.

History was making fast about the humble household in Cincinnati. In January of this eventful year Mrs. Stowe's third child, Henry Ellis, was born. The following June she writes to Miss May:

"Only think how long it is since I have written to you, and how changed I am since then — the mother of three children! Well, if I have not kept the reckoning of old times, let this last circumstance prove my apology, for I have been hand, heart, and head full since I saw you.

"Now to-day, for example: I will tell you what I had in my mind from dawn till dewy eve. In the first place I waked about half after four and thought, 'Bless me, how light it is! I must get out of bed and rap to wake Mina up, for breakfast must be ready at six o'clock this morning. So out of bed I jump and seize the tongs and pound, pound, pound, over poor Mina's sleepy head, charitably allowing her about half an hour to get waked up in, — that being the quantum of time it takes me, or used to. Well, then baby wakes, qua, qua, qua, and I give him his breakfast, dozing meanwhile and soliloquizing as follows: 'Now I must not forget to tell about the starch and dried apples ' — doze —' ah! um dear me! why does n't Mina get up?' 'I don't hear her' — doze — 'a um! I wonder if Mina has soap enough! I think there were two bars left on Saturday ' — doze again — I wake again, 'Dear me! broad daylight, I must get up and go down and see if Mina is getting breakfast.' Up I jump and up wakes baby, 'Now little boy be good, and let mother dress for she is in a hurry.' I get my frock half on, and baby by that time has kicked himself down off his pillow, and is crying and fisting the bedclothes in great order. I stop with one sleeve off and one on to settle matters with him. Having planted him bolt upright and gone all up and down the chamber bare-footed to get blankets and pillows to prop him up, I finish putting my frock on and hurry down to satisfy myself by actual observation that breakfast is in progress. Then back I come into the nursery, where, remembering that it is washing day, and that there is a great deal of work to be done, I set myself to sweeping and dusting, and setting to rights where there are three little mischiefs always pulling down as fast as one can set up.

"Then there are Miss H and Miss E, concerning whom Mary will furnish you with all suitable particulars, who are chattering, hallooing, or singing at the tops of their voices, as may suit their various states of mind, while the nurse is getting their breakfast ready.

"This meal being cleared away and Mr. Stowe dispatched to the market with various memoranda of provisions, etc., and the baby being washed and dressed, I begin to think what next must be done. I start to cut out some little dresses, have just calculated the length, and got one breadth torn off when Master Henry makes a doleful lip, and falls to crying with might and main. I catch him up and turning around, see one of his sisters flourishing the things out of my work-box in fine style....

"But let this suffice, for of such details as these are all my days made up. Indeed my dear I am a mere drudge, with few ideas beyond babies and housekeeping. As for thoughts, reflections, and sentiments, good lack! good lack!

"I suppose I am a dolefully uninteresting person at present, but I hope I shall grow young again one of these days, for it seems to me that matters cannot always stand exactly as they do now.

"Well, Georgy, this marriage is—yes, I will speak well of it, after all; for when I can stop and think long enough to discriminate my head from my heels, I must say I think myself a fortunate woman both in husband and children. My children I would not change for all the ease, pleasure, and leisure I could have without them. They are money on interest whose value will be constantly increasing."

In May, 1840, a second son was born, and named Frederick William, in memory of the sturdy Prussian King, for whom Professor Stowe cherished an unbounded admiration. In December of the same year Mrs. Stowe writes to Miss May that for a year she has written nothing except an occasional business letter. For months she could not bear the least light and was confined to her bed with severe neuralgic pain in face and eyes. Yet she persistently looks on the bright side of it all and reflects that, although she has been ill six months out of twelve, she has had Anna the best of nurses and a good home to be sick in, her children have thrived, and all things considered, her troubles have been only sufficient to keep her from loving this earth too well.

In 1843 she visits her sister Mary in Hartford, Connecticut, and while there, writes to her husband, confiding to him some of her cherished literary schemes. To this letter he replies with enthusiasm: "My dear, you must be a literary woman. It is so written in the book of fate. Make all your calculations accordingly. Get a good stock of health and brush up your mind. Drop the E out of your name. It only encumbers it, and interferes with the flow and euphony.

"Write yourself fully and always Harriet Beecher Stowe, which is a name euphonious, flowing, and full of meaning. Then my word for it, your husband will lift up his head in the gate and all your children will rise up and call you blessed."

To this she replies: "On the whole, my dear, if I choose to be a literary lady, I have, I think, as good a chance of making profit by it as any one I know of. But with all this I have my doubts as to whether I shall be able to do so.

"Our children are just coming to the age when everything depends on my efforts. They are delicate in health, and nervous and excitable, and need a mother's whole attention. Can I lawfully divide my attention by literary efforts?

"There is one thing I must suggest. If I am to write I must have a room to myself that shall be my room.... I intend to have a regular part of each day devoted to the children, and then I shall take them in there."

In his reply to this letter Professor Stowe continues: "You have it in your power by means of this little magazine, the *Souvenir* a new magazine to which Mrs. Stowe was the leading contributor), to form the mind of the West for the coming generation. It is just as I told you in my last letter. God has written it in his book that you must be a literary woman, and who are we that we should contend against God? You must therefore make all your calculations to spend the rest of your life with your pen."

The following winter was one of sickness and gloom. Typhoid fever raged among the students of the seminary, and the house of the president and those of the professors were turned in-

to hospitals. In July, 1843, a few weeks before the birth of her third daughter, Georgiana May, Mrs. Stowe was overwhelmed by a crushing blow that fell like a thunder-bolt out of a clear sky. Her brother, Rev. George Beecher, accidentally shot himself in his own garden. Of his funeral she writes: "And so it is at last; there must come a time when all the most heart-broken, idolizing love can give us is a coffin and a grave. After all, the deepest and most powerful argument for the religion of Christ is its power in times like this."

After three years filled with all imaginable troubles of poverty, sickness, and death, she writes in March, 1846: "For all that I have had trouble I can think of nothing but the greatness and richness of God's mercy to me in giving me such friends, and in always caring for us in every strait. There has been no day this winter when I have not had abundant reason to see this. Some friend has always stepped in to cheer and help so that I have wanted for nothing. My husband has developed wonderfully as a housefather and nurse. You would laugh to see him in his spectacles gravely marching the little troop in their nightgowns up to bed, tagging after them, as he says, 'like an old hen after a flock of ducks.'

"The money for my journey to the East has been sent in a wonderful manner. All this shows the care of our Father, and encourages me to rejoice and to hope in Him." This letter is an apt illustration of her never failing faculty for being strengthened instead of crushed by trials. The purpose of Mrs. Stowe's visit to the East was to try hydropathic treatment at Dr. Wessellhoff's Water Cure at Brattleboro, Vermont. Her allusion to the way funds were provided is explained in this letter received from her husband a few days after her departure: "I was greatly comforted by your brief letter from Pittsburg. When I returned from the steamer the morning you left, I found in the post-office a letter from Mrs. G. W. Bull of New York, inclosing fifty dollars on account of sickness in my family. There was another inclosing fifty dollars more from

a Mrs. Devereaux of Raleigh, North Carolina, besides some smaller sums from others. My heart went out to God in aspiration and gratitude. None of the donors so far as I know have I ever seen or heard of before."

When her water cure treatment is drawing to a close, Professor Stowe writes to her: " And now, my dear wife, I want you to come home as quick as you can. The fact is, I cannot live without you, and if we were not so prodigious poor, I would come for you at once. There is no woman like you in this wide world. Who else has so much talent with so little self-conceit; so much reputation with so little affectation; so much literature with so little nonsense; so much enterprise with so little extravagance; so much tongue with so little scold; so much sweetness with so little softness; so much of so many things and so little of so many other things." In reply Mrs. Stowe writes: "I told Belle that I did not know till I came away how much I was dependent upon you for information. There are a thousand favorite subjects on which I could talk with you better than with any one else. If you were not already my dearly loved husband, I should certainly fall in love with you." Unlike " the prophet in his own land," Mrs. Stowe was most emphatically appreciated in her own household long before the world knew her.

Just before her return from Brattleboro, Mrs. Stowe writes to her husband: "In returning to my family, from whom I have been so long separated, I am impressed with a new and solemn feeling of responsibility. It appears to me that I am not probably destined for long life; at all events, the feeling is strongly impressed upon my mind that a work is put into my hands which I must be earnest to finish shortly. It is nothing great or brilliant in the world's eye; it lies in one small family circle, of which I am called to be the central point." This letter was written only six years before the publication of "Uncle Tom's Cabin."

For six months after her return from this Water Cure her eyes were so affected that she could write very little. Her health improved, however, after the birth of her third son, Samuel Charles, in January, 1848.

Finally, the Professor breaks down and has in turn to seek health at Brattleboro. While he is there Mrs. Stowe writes to her friend that she is so crushed with cares as to be drained of all capacity for "thought, feeling, memory, or emotion." In conclusion she adds with a return to something of her old playfulness: "Well, Georgy, I am thirty-seven years old! I am glad of it. I like to grow old and have six children, and cares endless. I wish you could see me with my flock all around me. They sum up my cares, and were they gone I should ask myself, 'What now remains to be done?' They are my work over which I fear and tremble."

In 1849, while Professor Stowe was still in Brattleboro and Mrs. Stowe and the faithful Anna were struggling with the "cares endless" and the six children in Cincinnati, a terrible scourge of cholera descended upon the city. The disease was malignant and virulent. People fell dead in the streets. Coffins containing the bodies of the victims were often stacked up before the houses waiting for any sort of a vehicle to take them to a place of burial. The children enjoyed the excitement, and ran into the house continually with new bulletins as to the number of coffins borne past the house in the last half hour and other equally exhilarating particulars. Large heaps of coal burned day and night on the cross streets and in the public squares, and the air had a deadly oppressiveness that seemed to weigh like lead on brain and heart. The death roll rose to one hundred and sixteen in one day. And still all were well in the Stowe household, and the Death Angel had passed by the door. Then one hundred and twenty deaths in a day became no unusual record. People got accustomed to the situation. When neighbors met on the street they made themselves agreeable by reciting the number of deaths in this or that house. Cholera dietetics, cholera medicines, chloride of lime, and funerals became the staple of daily conversation. Serious and religious persons threw in such moral and spiritual reflec-

tions as seemed appropriate to the occasion.

Then little Samuel Charles and Henry were both taken sick. The little dog, Daisy, whom they all loved, and who loved them all, was taken with the dread disease, and died in f rightf id spasms in half an hour. Little Charley followed. Mrs. Stowe writes to her husband in Brattleboro: "At last it is over, and our dear little one is gone from us. He is now among the blessed. My Charley, my beautiful, loving, gladsome baby, so loving, so sweet, so full of life and strength — now lies shrouded pale and cold in the room below.... I write as if there were no sorrow like my sorrow, yet there has been in this city, as in the land of Egypt, scarce a house without its dead. This heart-break, this anguish, has been everywhere, and where it will end God only knows."

This was the grief of which she later said: "In those depths of sorrow which seemed to me immeasurable, it was my only prayer to God that such anguish might not be suffered in vain.... I felt that I could never be consoled for it, unless this crushing of my own heart might enable me to work out some great good to others." CHAPTER S
How "uncle Tom's Cabin" Was Built

As a very little girl Mrs. Stowe had heard of the horrors of slavery from her aunt, Mary Hubbard, who had married a planter from the West Indies, and been unable to live on her husband's plantation because her health was undermined by the mental anguish that she suffered at the scenes of cruelty and wretchedness she was compelled to witness. She returned to the United States, and made her home with the Beechers. Of her Mrs. Stowe writes: "What she saw and heard of slavery filled her with constant horror and loathing. I often heard her say that she frequently sat by her window in the tropical night, when all was still, and wished that the island might sink in the ocean, with all its sin and misery, and that she might sink with it. " The effect of such expressions on the mind of a sensitive child like Harriet Beecher may well be imagined.

When she was about twenty years old

she went to live in Cincinnati, on the very borders of a slave State, and frequently visited Kentucky slave plantations, where she saw negro slavery in that mild and patriarchal form in which she pictures it in the opening chapters of "Uncle Tom's Cabin." At the time the Beechers were living in Cincinnati, her brother Charles was driven nearly distracted by trying to appropriate to himself his father's Calvinistic theology, and the study of Edwards on the Will. Filled with fatalism and despair, he gave up all hope of ever being able to preach, left Cincinnati, and took a position as clerk in a wholesale commission house in New Orleans that did business with the Red River cotton plantations. It was from him that Mrs. Stowe obtained the character of Legree. No character in the whole book was drawn more exactly from life. Charles Beecher and a young Englishman who was his traveling companion, while on a Mississippi steamboat going from New Orleans to St. Louis, actually witnessed the scene where the Legree of real life showed his fist and boasted that it was "hard as iron knocking down niggers, and that he didn't bother with sick niggers, but worked his in with the crop."

The scene in "Uncle Tom's Cabin" in which the Senator takes Eliza into his carriage, after her wild flight over the Ohio River on the floating ice, and carries her on a dark and stormy night to a place of safety, is a description of an event that took place in Mrs. Stowe's own Cincinnati household.

She had in her family as a servant a young woman whose little boy was the original of the "little Harry" of the story. One day she came to Mrs. Stowe in great distress, and told her that her old master was in the city looking for her, and might at any moment appear and drag her back to slavery. That very night, dark and stormy though it was, Professor Stowe and Henry Ward Beecher, who was at that time a student in Lane Seminary, took the woman and her child in the family carriage over just such roads as are described in the book, and brought them to the lonely farmhouse of a man named Van Sant, who ran one of the stations of the underground railroad. As they drove up to the house, Van Sant came out with a lighted candle in his hand, shielding the light from his eyes with his immense palm.

Professor Stowe sang out: "Are you the man who will shelter a poor woman and her child from slave-catchers?"

"I rather think I am," answered the big, honest fellow.

"I thought so," exclaimed Professor Stowe,helping the woman out of the carriage. So character after character, and scene after scene, in "Uncle Tom's Cabin" might be traced to the actual events and persons that inspired them years before the faintest notion of writing such a book had ever entered Mrs. Stowe's mind.

It was early in the month of May of the year 1850 that Mrs. Stowe, on her way to Brunswick, Maine, reached the house of her brother, the Rev. Edward Beecher, in Boston. She was weary and physically exhausted with the long journey which she had been compelled to make alone with the whole charge of children, accounts, and baggage, pushing her way through hurrying crowds, looking out for trunks, and bargaining with expressmen and hackmen. Yet in Boston there was no rest for her. She had to buy furniture and household supplies and have them packed and ready for shipping by the Bath steamer, which she herself was to take the following week, as on the whole the easiest and cheapest way to reach Brunswick. She had to save in every imaginable way, and to keep a strict account of all money expended. As a result she was able to write her husband, who was ill in Cincinnati, that the whole expense of the journey from Cincinnati to Brunswick would be only a trifle more than seventy-six dollars.

She found her brother Edward and his wife greatly agitated over the Fugitive Slave Bill, which was at the time being debated in Congress. This law not only gave the slave-holder of the South the right to seek out and drag back into slavery any colored person that he claimed as his property, but commanded the people of the free States to assist in this pitiless business. Doctor Edward Beecher had been the intimate friend and supporter of Lovejoy, who had not long before been murdered by a pro-slavery mob for publishing an Anti-Slavery paper. The most frequent topic of conversation while Mrs. Stowe was in Boston was this proposed law, and as the result her soul was all on fire with indignation and grief over what she felt to be a new enormity and wrong about to be inflicted by the slave power on an innocent and defenseless race.

On the eve of her departure for Brunswick she wrote to her old friend of Hartford school days, Georgiana May, now Mrs. Sykes: "I am wearied and worn out with seeing to bedsteads, tables, chairs, mattresses, and with thinking about shipping my goods, and making out accounts, and I have my trunk yet to pack to go on board the Bath steamer this evening.

"I beg you to look up Brunswick on the map; it is about half a day's ride in the cars from Boston. I expect to reach there by the way of Bath by to-morrow forenoon. There I have a house engaged and kind friends who offer every hospitable assistance. Come, therefore, to see me, and we will have a long talk in the pine woods, and knit up the whole history from the place where we left it."

On her arrival in Brunswick, Mrs. Stowe was treated to an instructive if depressing lesson in New England weather. She says: "After a week of most incessant northeast storm, most discouraging and forlorn to the children, the sun has at length come out.... There is a fair wind blowing, and every prospect, therefore, that our goods will arrive from Boston, and that we shall be in our own house by next week."

In a letter written the following December to her sister-in-law, Mrs. George Beecher, we have in her own words a graphic and amusing picture of that first spring and summer in Brunswick: —

"Is it really true that snow is on the ground and Christmas coming, and I have not written unto thee, most dear sister? No, I don't believe it! I haven't been so naughty—it's all a mistake. Yes, written I must have, —and written I have, too, — in the night watches as I lay on my bed—such beautiful letters — I wish you had only gotten them; but by day it has been hurry, hurry, and drive, drive, drive! or else the calm of the sickroom, ever since last spring.

"... I put off writing when your letter first came because I meant to write you a long letter, — a full and complete one; and so the days slipped by, and became weeks, and then my little Charley came. l

"Sarah, when I look back, I wonder at myself, not that I forgot anything that I should remember, but that I have remembered anything. From the time that I left Cincinnati with my children to come forth to a country that I knew not of, almost to the present time, it has seemed that I could scarcely breathe, I was so pressed with care. My head dizzy with the whirl of railroads and steamboats; then ten days' sojourn in Boston, and a constant toil and hurry in buying my furniture and equipments; and then landing in Brunswick in the midst of a drizzly, inexorable northeast storm, and beginning the l Her seventh and last child, Charles Edward, born July 8,1850.

work of getting in order a deserted, dreary, damp old house. All day long, running from one thing to another, as for example thus: —

"'Mrs. Stowe, how shall I make this lounge, and what shall I cover the back with first?'

"*Mrs. Stowe.* With the coarse cotton in the closet.'

"*Woman.* 'Mrs. Stowe, there isn't anymore soap to clean the windows. Where shall I get soap?'

"*Mrs. Stowe.* 'Here, Hattie, run up to the store and get two bars.'

"' There is a man below wants to see Mrs. Stowe about the cistern.'

"' Before you go down, Mrs. Stowe, show me how to cover this round end of the lounge.'

"' There's a man up from the station, and he says that there is a box that has come for Mrs. Stowe, and it's coming up to the house; will you come down and see about it?'

"' Mrs. Stowe, don't go till you have shown the man how to nail the carpet in the corner. He's nailed it all crooked; what shall he do? The black thread is all used up; what shall I do about putting gimp on the back of that sofa? Mrs. Stowe, there is a man come with a lot of pails and tinware from Furbish; will you settle the bill now?'

"' Mrs. Stowe, here is a letter just come from Boston inclosing that bill of lading; the man wants to know what he shall do with the goods. If you will tell me what to say, I will answer the letter for you.'

"' Mrs. Stowe, the meat-man is at the door. Had n't we better get a little beef-steak or something for dinner?'

"' Shall Hattie go to Boardman's for some more black thread?'

"' Mrs. Stowe, this cushion is an inch too wide for the frame; what shall we do now?'

"' Mrs. Stowe, where are the screws of the black-walnut bedstead?'

"' Here's a man has brought in those bills for freight; will you settle them now?'

"'Mrs. Stowe, I don't understand using this great needle. I can't make it go through the cushion; it sticks in the cotton.'

"Then comes a letter from my husband, saying that he is sick abed, and all but dead; don't ever expect to see his family again; wants to know how I shall manage in case I am left a widow; knows that we shall get into debt and never get out; wonders at my courage; thinks that I am very sanguine; warns me to be prudent, as there won't be much to live on in case of his death, etc. , etc., etc. I read the letter, and poke it into the stove, and proceed....

"Some of my adventures were quite funny; as, for example, I had in my kitchen elect no sink, cistern, or any other water privileges, so I bought at the cotton factory two of the great hogsheads that they bring oil in, which here in Brunswick are often used for cisterns, and had them brought up in triumph to my yard, and was congratulating myself on my energy, when, lo and behold! it was discovered that there

was no cellar door except the one in the kitchen, which was truly a straight and narrow way down a long flight of stairs. Hereupon, as saith John Bunyan, 'I fell into a muse' — how to get my cisterns into my cellar. In the days of chivalry I might have got me a knight to make me a breach through the foundation walls; but that was not to be thought of now, and my oil hogsheads standing disconsolately in the yard seemed to reflect no great credit on my foresight. In this strait, I fell upon a real honest Yankee cooper, whom I besought, for the reputation of his craft and mine, to take my hogsheads in pieces, and carry them down in staves, and set them up again, which the worthy man actually accomplished in one fair summer forenoon, to the great astonishment of us Yankees. When my man came to put up the pump, he stared very hard to see my hogsheads thus translated and standing as innocently and quietly as could be in the cellar. Then I told him in a very quiet and mild way how I got them taken to pieces and put together again, just as if I had been always in the habit of doing such things.

"Professor Smith came down and looked very hard at them, and then said, ' Well, nothing can beat a willful woman!'

"In all my moving and fussing Mr. Titcomb has been my right-hand man. This same John Titcomb, my very good friend, is a character peculiar to Yankeedom. He is part owner and landlord of the house I rent, and connected by birth with all the best families in town,—a man of real intelligence and good education, a great reader, and quite a thinker.... Whenever a screw was loose, a nail to be driven, a lock to be mended, a pane of glass to be set,—and these cases were manifold, — he was always on hand. My sink, however, was no fancy job, and I believe that nothing but a very particular friendship would have moved him to undertake it.... How many times I have entered his shop, and seated myself in one of the old rocking-chairs, and first talked of the news of the day, the railroad, the last proceedings in Congress, the probabilities about

the millennium, and thus brought the conversation by little and little round to my sink; because, till the sink was done, the pump could not be put up, and we couldn't have any rain water. Sometimes my courage quite failed me to introduce the subject, and I would talk of everything else, turn and get out of the shop, and then come back, as if a thought had just struck my mind, and say: —

"'Mr. Titcomb, about that sink?'

"'Yes, ma'am; I was thinking about going down street this afternoon to look out stuff for it.'

"'Yes, sir, if you would be good enough to get it done as soon as possible; we are in great need of it.'

"' I think there's no hurry. I believe we are going to have a dry time now, so that you could not catch any water, and you won't need the pump at present.'

"These negotiations extended from the first of June to the first of July, and at last my sink was completed, as also was a new house-spout, concerning which I had divers communings with Deacon Dunning of the Baptist Church.

"Also, during this time, good Mrs. Mitchell and myself made two sofas, or lounges, a barrel-chair, divers bedspreads, pillowcases, pillows, bolsters, mattresses; we painted rooms; we revarnished furniture; we—what *didn't* we do?

"Then came Mr. Stowe, and then came the eighth of July, and my little Charley. I was really glad for an excuse to lie in bed, for I was full tired, I can assure you. Well, I was what folks call very comfortable for two weeks, when my nurse had to leave me.

"During this time I have employed my leisure hours in making up my engagements with newspaper editors. I have written more than anybody or I myself would have thought to be possible. I have taught an hour a day in our school, and I have read two hours every evening to the children. The children study English history in school, and I am reading Scott's historical novels with them in their order. To-night I finish 'The Abbot,' and shall begin 'Kenilworth' next week. Yet I am con stantly pursued and haunted by the idea that I don't do anything.

"Since I began this note, I have been called off at least a dozen times: once for the fish-man, to buy a codfish; once to see a man who had brought me some barrels of apples; once to see a book agent; then to Mrs. Upham's to see about a drawing I promised to make for her; then to nurse the baby; then into the kitchen to make a chowder for dinner; and now I am at it again, for nothing but deadly determination enables me ever to write; it is rowing against wind and tide."

While all this was going on in Brunswick, her brother's family in Boston were consumed with righteous indignation over the workings of the Fugitive Slave Law.

Mrs. Stowe received letter after letter from Mrs. Edward Beecher and other friends, picturing the heartrending scenes which were the inevitable results of the enforcement of this inhuman law. Cities were better adapted than the country to the work of capturing escaped slaves, and Boston, called the "Cradle of Liberty," opened her doors to slave-hunters. The sorrow and anguish caused was indescribable. Familieswere broken up. Someof the hunted ones hid in garrets and cellars. Others fled to the wharves and embarking in ships, sailed for Europe. Others tried to make their way to Canada. One poor fellow who had long been supporting his family well as a crockery merchant, when he got word that his master was in the city seeking him, set out in midwinter to walk to Canada, as he dared not take a public conveyance, and froze both his feet on the journey. They had to be amputated.

Mrs. Edward Beecher, writing of this period to Mrs. Stowe's youngest son, says: —

"I had been nourishing an Anti-Slavery spirit since Lovejoy was murdered for publishing in his paper articles against slavery and intemperance, when our home was in Illinois. These terrible things that were going on in Boston were well calculated to rouse up this spirit. What can I do? I thought. Not much myself, but I know one who can. So I wrote several letters to your mother, telling her of the various heartrending events caused by the enforcement of the Fugitive Slave Law. I remember distinctly saying in one of them: 'Now, Hattie, if I could use a pen as you can, I would write something that would make this whole nation feel what an accursed thing slavery is!'"

A daughter of Mrs. Stowe well remembered her whole life long the scene in the little parlor in Brunswick when this letter was received and read. Mrs. Stowe read it aloud to the assembled family, and when she came to the words, "I would write something that would make this whole nation feel what an accursed thing slavery is," rising from her chair, and crushing the letter in her hand, she exclaimed, with an expression on her face that stamped itself permanently on the minds of her children: —

"God helping me, I will write something. I will if I live."

This purpose, though then definitely formed, could not be immediately carried out. In a letter written in the month of December, 1850, she refers to the matter in a way that shows how it weighed upon her mind: —

"Tell sister Katy that I thank her for her letter, and will answer it. As long as the baby sleeps with me nights, I can't do much at anything; but I will do it at last. I will write that thing if I live.

"What are folks in general saying about the slave law, and the stand taken by Boston ministers in general, except Edward?

"To me it is incredible, amazing, mournful! I feel that I should be willing to sink with it, were all this sin and misery to sink in the sea.... I wish father would come on to Boston and preach on the Fugitive Slave Law, as he once preached on the slave trade, when I was a little girl in Litchfield. I sobbed aloud in one pew, and Mrs. Judge Reeve in another. I wish some Martin Luther would arise to set this community right. "

At this time Mrs. Stowe was not an Abolitionist, nor did she ever become one after the Garrisonian type. She remembered hearing her father say about Garrison and Wendell Phillips that they were like men that would burn their houses down to get rid of the rats. She was virtually in sympathy with her father on the subject of slavery, and had unlimited confidence in his judgment. What Doctor Beecher thought of the Abolitionists, he expressed with a vigor and clarity that left no doubt as to his position. He said: —

"I regard the whole Abolition movement, under its most influential leaders, with its distinctive maxims and modes of feeling, and also the whole temper, principles, and action of the South in justification of slavery, as a singular instance of infatuation permitted by Heaven for purposes of national retribution. God never raised up such men as Garrison and others like him as the ministers of his mercy for purposes of peaceful reform, but only as the fit and fearful ministers of his vengeance upon a people incorrigibly wicked."

These words were written in 1838, and show how true was the prophetic sense of Lyman Beecher. Garrison was at this time preaching secession and praying for the dissolution of the Union, and calling the Constitution of the United States a " Covenant with Death and an Agreement with Hell." No true Abolitionist should vote or have anything to do with the Government as then constituted. In this sense, neither Mrs. Stowe nor her husband were Abolitionists. Mrs. Stowe wished to be more than fair to the South. She intended to be generous. She made two of Uncle Tom's three masters men of good character, amiable, kind, and generous. She tried to show that the fault was not with the Southern people, but with the system. A friend of hers, who had many friends in the South, wrote to her: "Your book is going to be the great pacificator; it will unite North and South." Mrs. Stowe did not expect that the Abolitionists would be satisfied with the story, but she confidently expected that it would be favorably received in the South. Great was her surprise, then, when from the whole South arose a storm of abuse, while the

Abolitionists received her with open arms. Mr. Garrison wrote: "I measure the value of Abolition literature by the abuse it brings. Since 'Uncle Tom's Cabin ' has been published, all the defenders of slavery have let me alone and are spending their strength in abusing you."

It was in the winter of 1850 that she wrote to her husband, who was in Cincinnati, giving a picture of her lif e in the old, wind-swept castle of a house in Brunswick.

"Sunday night I rather watched than slept. The wind howled, and the house rocked, just as our old Litchfield house used to do.... I am projecting a sketch for the *Era* on the capacity of liberated blacks to take care of themselves. Can't you find out for me how much Willie Watson has paid for the liberation of his friends? Get any items of that kind that you can pick up in Cincinnati....

"When I have a headache, and feel sick, as I do to-day, there is actually not a place in the house where I can lie down and take a nap without being disturbed. Overhead is the schoolroom; next door is the dining-room, and the girls practice there two hours a day on the piano. If I lock my door and lie down, some one is sure to be rattling the latch before two minutes have passed....

"There is no doubt in my mind that our expenses this year will come two hundred dollars, if not three, beyond our salary. We shall be able to come through notwithstanding; but I don't want to feel obliged to work as hard every year as I have this. I can earn four hundred dollars a year by writing; but I don't want to feel that I must, when weary with teaching the children, and tending the baby, and buying provisions, and mending dresses, and darning stockings, sit down and write a piece for some paper."

Again she writes: —

"Ever since we left Cincinnati to come here, the good hand of God has been visibly guiding our way. Through what difficulties have we been brought! Though we knew not where means were to come from, yet means have been furnished at every step of the way, and in

every time of need. I was just in some discouragement with regard to my writing, thinking that the editor of the *Era* was overstocked with contributors and would not want my services another year, and, lo, he sends me one hundred dollars, and ever so many good words with it. Our income this year will be seventeen hundred dollars in all, and I hope to bring our expenses within thirteen hundred." At the time she wrote these words she had no idea or conception of writing such a serial story as " Uncle Tom's Cabin." It is true that she was determined to write something to make the whole nation feel that slavery was an "accursed thing," but what she was to write had not, in the dimmest outline, as yet formed itself in her mind.

About the last of January, 1850, she went to Boston to visit her brother Edward, and there she met, for the first time, the Rev. Josiah Henson. She heard his story of his escape from slavery. He remembered seeing his own father lying on the ground, bruised, bloody, and dying from the blows of a white overseer, because, mere slave and "nigger" that he was, he had pretended that the mother of his children was his wife, and had tried to defend her from an indecent assault that this same overseer had attempted on her person. What struck her most forcibly in Henson's story was the sweet Christian spirit of the man, as manifested even when he spoke of injuries calculated to rouse a human being to a frenzy of vindictive revengefulness.

Shortly after this visit to Boston, Mrs. Stowe was seated in her pew in the college church at Brunswick during the communion service. She was alone with her children, her husband having gone away to deliver a course of lectures. Suddenly, like the unrolling of a picture scroll, the scene of the death of Uncle Tom seemed to pass before her. At the same time, the words of Jesus were sounding in her ears: "Inasmuch as ye have done it unto one of the least of these my brethren, ye have done it unto me." It seemed as if the crucified, but now risen and glorified Christ, were speaking to her through the poor black man, cut and bleeding under the blows

of the slave whip. She was affected so strongly that she could scarcely keep from weeping aloud.

That Sunday afternoon she went to her room, locked the door, and wrote out, substantially as it appears in the published editions, the chapter called " The Death of Uncle Tom." As sufficient paper was not at hand, she wrote a large part of it in pencil on some brown paper in which groceries had been delivered. It seemed to her as if what she wrote was blown through her mind as with the rushing of a mighty wind. In the evening she gathered her little family about her and read them what she had written. Her two little boys of ten and twelve burst into tears, sobbing out, "Oh, mama, slavery is the most cruel thing in the world!" This was the beginning of " Uncle Tom's Cabin." She was not apparently conscious of what she had done, nor did she immediately consider making use of the fragment she had written.

In an introduction to "Uncle Tom's Cabin," written late in life, Mrs. Stowe refers to the incident of Eliza's flight over the ice as the first "salient point" in the story. She also refers to the incident as though she had learned of it for the first time in the pages of an Anti-Slavery magazine. As a matter of fact, it was an actual occurrence during her residence in Ohio. She had known and had often talked with the very man who helped Eliza up the bank of the river. This was years before she had ever thought of writing such a book as " Uncle Tom's Cabin." No one is entirely reliable as a witness to events long past. Furthermore, in Mrs. Stowe's case, the great burden of so many overtaxed years had by this time made her memory more treacherous than she or her family realized. Professor Stowe, who was still living at the time, called attention to these and other inaccuracies, but for some reason not known they were never corrected.

At the time this occurred Mrs. Stowe's mind was apparently so absorbed by pressing domestic duties that what she had written was laid one side and for the time forgotten. She did not even show it to her husband, on his return from his lecture trip. One day she found him dissolved in tears over the bits of brown paper on which she had written the first words of "Uncle Tom's Cabin." Largely at his suggestion, she determined to write a serial story, the climax of which was to be the death of Uncle Tom. Some weeks slipped by before she wrote the first instalment of the proposed novel. In the mean time she had written to Gamaliel Bailey, editor of the *National Era,* an Abolition paper published in Washington, District of Columbia, that she contemplated a serial story under the title, " Uncle Tom's Cabin, or Life Among the Lowly," and asking if it would be acceptable to the *Era.*

Neither Mrs. Stowe nor her husband had the remotest idea of the unique power and interest of the story that was being written. Nor, indeed, did it dawn upon either of them until after the publication of the first edition in book form. Professor Stowe was a very emotional man, and was accustomed to water his wife's literary efforts liberally with his tears; so the fact that he had wept over the bits of brown paper had for them no unusual portent. As to pecuniary gain, he often expressed the hope that she would make money enough by the story to buy a new silk dress.

It was a jolly, rollicking household in Brunswick, and Mrs. Stowe was herself full of fun. It was during the writing of "Uncle Tom's Cabin" that there occurred the following incident characteristic of the family life. Professor Stowe was at heart one of the most genial of men; but, being of an exceedingly nervous temperament, he was liable to go off at half cock on the slightest provocation, and become for the time being pleasantly peppery. One day he bought a dozen eggs to set under a brooding hen, with a view to producing an unusually fine lot of chickens. Without disclosing his purpose he hid the eggs, as he thought securely, in the wood-shed. One of the children discovered them, and bore them in triumph into the house. Mrs. Stowe was on the point of sending to the store for eggs, and look-

ing upon this discovery as providential, took them and had them cooked. Upon returning from one of his lectures, the Professor felt himself the most abused of men when he sought his eggs and found them not, and vented his wrath upon his innocent household in a form at once dramatic and picturesque. Then off he went to another lecture, in a forbidding frame of mind.

"Pa's mad!" observed one of the children.

"I tell you what we 'll do, children; when he comes back to dinner, we will make him laugh and he 'll get all over it," said Mrs. Stowe, with a roguish twinkle in her eye. The Professor returned, and found the dinner on the table, ready and waiting, but not one of the family visible. While speculating on this unusual state of affairs, he heard a very human imitation of the cackling of hens proceeding from the wood-shed. It made up in vigor what it lacked in genuineness. On investigation, he found his wife and all the children, and even Rover, the dog, perched on a beam, after the manner peculiar to hens. He burst into laughter, and they all trooped into the house and had a very jolly time at dinner.

"Uncle Tom's Cabin" began as a serial in the *National Era,* June 5, 1851, and in July of the same year Mrs. Stowe wrote as follows to Frederick Douglass: "You may perhaps have noticed in your editorial readings a series of articles that I am furnishing for the *Era,* under the title of 'Uncle Tom's Cabin, or Life Among the Lowly.'

"In the course of my story the scene will fall upon a cotton plantation. I am very desirous, therefore, to gain information from one who has been an actual laborer on one, and it occurred to me that in the circle of your acquaintance there might be one who would be able to communicate to me such information as I desire. I have before me an able paper written by a Southern planter, in which the details and *modus operandi* are given from his point of sight. I am anxious to have something more from another standpoint, I wish to make a picture that shall be graphic and true

to nature in its details. Such a person as Henry Bibb, if in the country, might give me just the kind of information I desire. You may possibly know of some other person. I will subjoin to this letter a list of questions, which in that case you will do me a favor by inclosing to the individual, with the request that he will at earliest convenience answer them...."

Then, after a vigorous defense of churches and ministers whom Douglass had assailed, she continues: —

"I am a minister's daughter, and a minister's wife, and I have had six brothers in the ministry (one is in Heaven); I certainly ought to know something of the feelings of ministers on this subject.

"I was a child in 1820, when the Missouri question was agitated, and one of the strongest and deepest impressions on my mind was that made by my father's sermons and prayers, and the anguish of his soul for the poor slave at that time. I remember his preaching drawing tears down the hardest faces of the old farmers of his congregation.

"I remember his prayers, morning and evening, in the family for 'poor, oppressed, bleeding Africa,' that the time of her deliverance might come; prayers offered with strong crying and tears, prayers that indelibly impressed my heart, and made me, what I am, the enemy of all slavery....

"Every brother I have has be#en in his sphere a leading Anti-Slavery man. One of them, Edward, was to the last the bosom friend and counselor of Lovejoy. As for myself and my husband, we have for the last seventeen years lived on the border of a slave state, and we have never shrunk from the fugitives, and we have helped them with all we had to give. I have received the children of liberated slaves into a family school, and taught them with my own children..."

In a letter written to Mrs. Follen in February, 1853, after the publication of "Uncle Tom's Cabin," Mrs. Stowe throws additional light on the way in which that Cabin was built out of the sorrows and experiences of her own life. Speaking of her life in Cincinnati, she writes: —

"A number of poor families settled in our vicinity, from whom we could occasionally obtain domestic service. About a dozen families of liberated slaves were among the number, and they became my favorite resort in cases of emergency. If any one wants to see a black face look handsome, let them be left, as I have been, in feeble health, in oppressive weather, with a sick baby in arms, and two or three other little ones in the nursery, and not a servant in the whole house to do a single turn. Then, if they could see my good old Aunt Frankie coming with her honest, bluff, black face, her long strong arms, her chest as big and stout as a barrel, and her hilarious, hearty laugh, perfectly delighted to take one's washing, and do it at a fair price, they would appreciate the beauty of black people. My cook, Eliza Buck, was a regular epitome of slave life in herself,—fat, gentle, easy, loving, and lovable, always calling my very modest house and dooryard 'The Place,' as if it had been a plantation with seven hundred hands on it. She had lived through the whole sad story of a Virginia-raised slave's life. In her youth she must have been a very handsome mulatto girl. Her voice was sweet, and her manners refined and agreeable. She was raised in a good family as a nurse and seamstress. When the family became embarrassed, she was suddenly sold on to a plantation in Louisiana. She has often told me how, without any warning, she was suddenly forced into a carriage, and saw her little mistress screaming and stretching her arms from a window toward her as she was driven away. She has told me of scenes on the Louisiana plantation, and she has often been out at night by stealth, ministering to poor slaves who had been mangled and lacerated by the lash. Then she was sold into Kentucky, and her last master was the father of all her children. On this point she always maintained a delicacy and reserve that seemed to me remarkable. She always called him her husband, and it was not till after she had lived with me some

years that I discovered the real nature of the connection. I shall never forget how sorry I felt for her, nor my feelings at her humble apology,' You know, Mrs. Stowe, slave women cannot help themselves.' She had two very pretty quadroon daughters, with her hair and eyes, — interesting children, whom I instructed in the family school with my own children. Time would fail to tell you all that I learned incidentally of the slave system in the history of various slaves who came into my family, and of the underground railway, which, I may say, ran through our house."

Later in this same letter she connects intimately the writing of "Uncle Tom's Cabin" with her own griefs and bereavements. "I have been the mother of seven children, the most beautiful and most loved of whom lies buried near my Cincinnati residence. It was at his dying bed and at his grave that I learned what a poor slave mother may feel when her child is torn away from her. In these depths of sorrow, which seemed to me immeasurable, it was my only prayer to God that such anguish might not be suffered in vain. There were circumstances about his death of such peculiar bitterness, of what seemed almost cruel suffering, that I felt that I could never be consoled for it, unless this crushing of my own heart might enable me to work out some great good to others. I allude to this here, for I have often felt that much that is in that book, 'Uncle Tom's Cabin,' had its root in the awful scenes and bitter sorrows of that summer. It has left now, I trust, no trace on my mind except a deep compassion for the sorrowful, especially for mothers who are separated from their children."

Such is Mrs. Stowe's own account of where and how she gained the material and the inspiration for writing "Uncle Tom's Cabin." The book came as the ripe fruit of her whole life experience up to the time when she wrote the first words on the rough pieces of brown paper.

It was written mostly in Brunswick, Maine. Some of the chapters were written in Boston, while she was visiting her brother, Edward Beecher, and part

of the concluding chapter in Andover. Begun as a serial in the National Era, June 5, 1851, and announced to run for but three months, it was not completed till April 1, 1852, and was published in book form March 20 of the same year.

John P. Jewett, a young publisher of Boston, made overtures for the publication of "Uncle Tom's Cabin" in book form long before it was finished as a serial in the National Era. The contract was finally signed March 13,1852. Not long before this, Mr. Jewett wrote Mrs. Stowe, expressing the fear that she was making the story too long for one volume. He reminded her that the subject was unpopular, and that, while one short volume might possibly sell, two volumes might prove a fatal obstacle to the success of the book. Mrs. Stowe replied that she did not make the story, that the story made itself, and that she could not stop till it was done.

Mr. Jewett offered her either ten per cent on all sales, or half profits with half the risk in case the venture proved unprofitable. Professor and Mrs. Stowe had for their business adviser Mr. Philip Greeley, who had formerly been Collector of the Port of Boston and was then a member of Congress. On this matter, without reading the story, he strongly advised them to accept the ten per cent on all sales, and to take no risk whatever in the enterprise. He reasoned that the subject was very unpopular, and that a book written by a woman could not be expected to have a very large sale in any case. Doctor Stowe took the first copy of the first edition to the railroad station and put it into Mr. Greeley's hands just as he was leaving for Washington. Greeley was a sedate and selfcontained man, — a characteristically unemotional New Englander. Afterward he wrote to Professor Stowe that he began the book shortly after the train pulled out of the station, and that as he read he began to cry. He was humiliated. He had never before shed tears over a novel, still less over the work of a woman. Yet after he had begun it, he could not stop reading, nor could he keep the tears back as he read. Consequently, on reaching Springfield, he left the train and went to a hotel, took a room, and sat up till he finished the book in the early hours of the morning.

CHAPTER VI FROM OBSCURITY TO FAME
One apparently trivial incident in Mrs. Stowe's life ploughed itself so deeply into her memory that it left an enduring impression. It was at the time when she, with her five little children, was making her way alone from Cincinnati to Brunswick, bargaining with hackmen and baggage men, amid the confusion of hurrying crowds and the rush and roar of steamboats and trains. Unconscionably early one morning she found herself at a railroad station where she must wait three weary hours for the next train. She sat on her baggage, her children grouped about her, looking, according to her own testimony, extremely shabby and disconsolate. In this attitude she was discovered by a brisk and self-important little station agent, who evidently regarded her with suspicion as an undesirable citizen, and questioned her with extreme asperity of manner as to where she came from and where she was going. When she had answered quietly and briefly, the peremptory little functionary strode away and left her with an unreasonable but keen consciousness of her own insignificance. This was Harriet Beecher Stowe two years before the writing of " Uncle Tom's Cabin." That this brisk little watch-dog of respectability felt called upon to bark at her struck her sense of humor, and she often told of it with a twinkle in her eye. George Eliot has somewhere remarked that even the great Sir Isaac Newton surveying his countenance in the convex lense of a highly polished door knob would have been compelled to rest satisfied "with the facial angles of a bumpkin," but Harriet Beecher Stowe was not inclined to seek consolations of this nature at the expense of the brisk little station agent. On the contrary, the Apostle Paul himself could not have had a keener sense of his own weakness according to the flesh than had Mrs. Stowe. "So you want to know something about what sort of a woman I am!" she writes Mrs. Follen immediately after the publication

of " Uncle Tom's Cabin." "Well, if this is any object, you shall have statistics free of charge. To begin, then, I am a little bit of a woman, — somewhat more than forty, just as thin and dry as a pinch of snuff; never very much to look at in my best days, and looking like a used-up article now." This was the Harriet Beecher Stowe that the aggressive little station master found sitting on her luggage with her five children about her in the dim and misty dawn of an April morning in the year 1850.

Two years later this little woman "just as thin and dry as a pinch of snuff" had written a story called "Uncle Tom's Cabin." Looking back on that time more than thirty years afterwards, she writes: "' Uncle Tom's Cabin' was published March 20, 1852. The despondency of the author as to whether anybody would read or attend to her appeal was soon dispelled. Ten thousand copies were sold in a few days, and over three hundred thousand within a year, and eight power presses running day and night were barely able to keep pace with the demand for it. It was read everywhere, apparently, and by everybody, and she soon began to hear echoes of sympathy from all over the land. The indignation, the pity, the distress, that had long weighed upon her soul seemed to pass off from her and into the readers of the book."

It was like the kindling of a mighty conflagration, the sky was all aglow with the resistless tide of emotion that swept all before it and even crossed the broad ocean, till it seemed as if the whole world scarcely thought or talked of anything else. Then, multitudes began to ask who had done this thing? Who had set the world on fire? And, lo, there stood outlined against the great light "a little bit of a woman... just as thin and dry as a pinch of snuff."

That was Harriet Beecher Stowe. Like the noise of mighty winds, like the rushing of the waters, there arose from the earth a tumult of human voices. There was the voice of weeping, and the cry of those who said, "Can nothing be done to banish this accursed thing from off the face of the earth?" Then

followed the outburst of rage, hatred, and defiance. The hells were stirred to their very depths, and belched obscenity and profanity.

There came to Mrs. Stowe letters " so curiously compounded of blasphemy, cruelty, and obscenity that their like could only be expressed by John Bunyan's account of the speech of Apollyon: 'He spake as a dragon.'"

Let us hear again what Mrs. Stowe herself said: —

"For a time, after it ' Uncle Tom's Cabin' was issued, it seemed to go by acclamation. From quarters most unexpected, from all political parties, came a most unbroken chorus of approbation. I was very much surprised, for I knew the explosive nature of the subject. It was not till the sale had run to over a hundred thousand copies that reaction began, and the reaction was led off by the London *Times*. Instantly, as by a preconcerted signal, all papers of a certain class began to abuse; and some who had at first issued articles entirely commendatory now issued others equally depreciatory. Religious papers, notably the New York *Observer,* came out and denounced the book as anti-Christian, anti-evangelical, resorting even to personal slander of the author as a means of diverting attention from the work.

"My book... is as much under an interdict in some parts of the South as the Bible in Italy. It is not allowed in the book-stores, and the greater part of the people hear of it and me only through grossly caricatured representations in the papers, with garbled extracts from the book.

"A cousin residing in Georgia this winter says that the prejudice against me is so strong that she dares not have my name appear on the outside of her letters, and that very amiable and excellent people have asked her if such as I could be received into reputable society at the North.

"The storm of feeling that the book raises in Italy, Germany, and France is all good, though truly 'tis painful for us Americans to bear."

Within a year the obscure little woman had become a figure of international importance. Not only had her book been universally read, but it had been taken so seriously as to become a great political and moral force in the world.

How was she herself affected by this dazzlingly sudden transition from the quiet obscurity in which she had hitherto passed her days to this prodigious fame? One might almost say that she was not affected at all! As Mrs. Fields has most truly said in the "Life and Letters ": "The sense that a great work had been accomplished through her only made her, if possible, less self-conscious." No one who knew Mrs. Stowe will deny that she possessed the artistic temperament, but she was not preeminently an artist. She never looked at things solely from the aesthetic point of view. In the daughter of Lyman Beecher, the artist was dominated by the preacher and reformer. Hence, "Uncle Tom's Cabin" was to her a sermon hurled against a great moral evil. Never once does she display the artist's quiet satisfaction in a work of art done for art's sake. No! far from it! She is determined that the world shall be convinced that she has spoken the truth.

With this aim in view, she sets herself immediately to write the "Key to Uncle Tom's Cabin"! In those first months after the publication of the book she is too much in earnest to think of herself at all, any more than old Lyman Beecher thought of himself when, with tears in his eyes, and three or more pairs of spectacles on top of his head, he urged sinners to repentance. While at work on the "Key" she writes to Mrs. Follen: "I am now writing a work which will contain perhaps an equal amount of matter with 'Uncle Tom's Cabin.' It will contain all the facts and documents on which that story was founded, an immense body of facts, reports of trials, legal documents, and testimony of people now living South, which will more than confirm every statement in Uncle Tom's Cabin.'

"I must confess that till I began the examination of facts to write this book, much as I thought I knew before, I had not begun to measure the depths of the abyss.

"The law records of courts and judicial proceedings are so incredible as to fill me with amazement whenever I think of them. It seems to me that the book cannot but be felt, and, coming upon the sensibility awakened by the other, do something.

"I suffer exquisitely in writing these things. It may be truly said, I write them with my heart's blood. Many times in writing' Uncle Tom's Cabin' I thought my health would fail utterly; but I prayed earnestly that God would help me till I got through, and still I am pressed beyond measure and beyond strength....

"It seems so odd and dreamlike that so many persons desire to see me, and now I cannot help thinking that they will think when they do, 'that God hath chosen the weak things of the world.'"

As her renown flowed in upon her from without, it was constantly met by that deeper and stronger tide which welled up from the deeps of her own soul. Professor Stowe had at this time accepted a chair at the Andover Theological Seminary in Massachusetts. She writes to him from Andover, speaking of the home that they are to have there.

"It seems almost too good to be true, that we are to have such a house, in such a beautiful place, and to live here among all these agreeable people, where everybody seems to love you so much, and think so much of you.

"I am almost afraid to accept it, and should not, did I not see the Hand that gives it all, and know that it is both firm and true.

"He knows if it is best for us, and His blessing addeth no sorrow therewith. I cannot describe to you the constant under-current of love and joy and peace ever flowing through my soul. I am so happy — so blessed!"

It was this undercurrent of love, joy, and peace that, about this time, found expression in that hymn by which Mrs. Stowe is perhaps as favorably known as by anything she wrote: —

Still, still, with Thee when purple morning breaketh,
When the bird waketh, and the shadows flee,
Fairer than morning, lovelier than the daylight,
Dawns the sweet consciousness I am with Thee.

One month after the publication of "Uncle Tom's Cabin " she writes to her husband: "It is not fame nor praise that contents me. I seem never to have needed love so much as now. I long to hear you say how much you love me."

There could be no truer picture of her inner life than she herself has given in that restful hymn: —

When winds are raging o'er the upper ocean,
And billows wild contend with angry roar,
'T is said far down beneath the wild commotion,
That peaceful stillness reigneth evermore.

So this woman, whose name was on every tongue, whose words were being translated into nearly every language and read in every land, lived in the midst of it all, hid as in a pavilion from the strife of tongues. So above and beyond it all was she, that it seemed but trivial to her who realized so intensely how "God's greatness flows about our incompleteness, and about our restlessness his rest."

The work on the "Key" completed, Professor and Mrs. Stowe accepted the invitation of the friends of the cause of emancipation in England to visit that country as their guest. When they landed at Liverpool, Mrs. Stowe was astonished to find a crowd waiting at the pier, — so little had it ever dawned upon her that she was a person of importance. "I had an early opportunity of making an acquaintance with my English brethren; for, much to my astonishment, I found quite a crowd on the wharf, and we walked up to our carriage through a long lane of people, bowing, and looking very glad to see us." She left Liverpool " with a heart a little tremulous and excited by the vibration of an atmosphere of universal sympathy and kindness." At Lockerbie, it is with a strange kind of thrill "she hears her name inquired for in the Scottish accent. Men, women, and children are gathered, and hand after hand is presented with the hearty greeting: 'Ye 're welcome to Scotland.'" Of the many kindnesses offered her that she could not accept or return, she says: "For all these kindnesses what could I give in return? There was scarcely time for even a grateful thought on each. People have often said to me that it must have been an exceeding bore. For my part, I could not think of regarding it so. It only oppressed me with an unutterable sadness." She writes of her visit to the Edinburgh Cathedral: "As I saw the way to the cathedral blocked up by a throng of people that had come out to see me, I could not help saying, 'What went ye out for to see: a reed shaken with the wind?' In fact, I was so worn out that I could hardly walk through the building. The next morning I was so ill as to need a physician." Everywhere her life is a constant fight with physical exhaustion. She consoles herself with the reflection: "Everybody seems to understand how good-for-nothing I am; and yet, with all this consideration, I have been obliged to keep my room and bed for a good part of the time. Of the multitudes that have called, I have seen scarcely any." She reflects in this connection, —

"What a convenience in sight-seeing it would be if one could have a relay of bodies, as of clothes, and slip from one into the other."

Nothing pleased her so much as the sympathy and appreciation everywhere shown by the working people. She speaks with genuine pleasure of putting her hand "into the great prairie of a palm" of one of the Duke of Argyle's farmers who had read " Uncle Tom's Cabin," and walked many miles to shake the hand of the author. She writes of the journey through Scotland: "We rode through several villages after this, and were met everywhere with a warm welcome. What pleased me was that it was not mainly from the literary, or the rich, or the great, but the plain, common people. The butcher came out of his stall, and the baker from his shop, the miller dusty with flour, the blooming, comely young mother, with her baby in

her arms, all smiling and bowing, with that hearty, intelligent, friendly look, as if they knew we should be glad to see them." To her the conventional was trivial and unimportant. She reached out instinctively to grasp those organic elements of human nature that are common to cultivated and uncultivated, rich and poor alike. It was the chord of the universal human which she had struck so powerfully in " Uncle Tom's Cabin" that was ringing in the hearts of these simple, sturdy people when they instinctively greeted her as their friend. She had appealed to humanity, and humanity was responding to the call. Only sheer exhaustion forced her to decline invitations from the workingmen of Dundee and Glasgow to attend receptions given in her honor. After one such public reception, where she was long and lustily cheered, her reflection is: "After all, I consider that these cheers and this applause are Scotland's voice to America, a recognition of the brotherhood of the nations."

Of her multitudinous engagements on this tour, which she had ingenuously looked forward to as a vacation, she writes: "As to all engagements, I am in a state of happy acquiescence, having resigned myself as a very tame lion into the hands of my keepers. Whenever the time comes for me to try to do anything, I try to behave myself as well as I can, which, as Dr. Young says, is all that an angel could do under the same circumstances." To find herself in the company of very distinguished people excites her sense of humor, and she laughs to herself: "Oh, isn't this funny, to see poor little me with all the great ones of the earth?" She writes to her husband from London about a concert at Stafford House: "The next day from my last letter came off Miss Greenfield's concert, of which I send a card. *You see in what company they have put your poor little wife!* Funny — isn't it? Well, the Hons. and the Right Hons. all were there, and I sat by Lord Carlisle."

The most notable event in which Mrs. Stowe was the central figure during this her first visit to England was the reception given her by the Duke and Duchess

of Sutherland at Stafford House, on the occasion when Lord Shaftesbury presented to her, in behalf of the women of England, an address of welcome and appreciation. Of this Mrs. Stowe writes: "When the Duchess appeared, I thought she looked handsomer by daylight than in the evening. She received us with the same warm and simple kindness which she had shown before.... Among the first that entered were the members of the family, the Duke and Duchess of Argyle, Lord and Lady Blantyre, the Marquis and Marchioness of Stafford, and Lady Emma Campbell. Then followed Lord Shaftesbury with his beautiful lady, and her father and mother, Lord and Lady Palmerston. Lord Palmerston is of middle height, with a keen dark eye and black hair streaked with gray. There is something peculiarly alert and vivacious about all his movements; in short, his appearance perfectly answers to what we know of him from his public life. One has a strange, mythological feeling about the existence of people of whom one hears for many years without ever seeing them. While talking with Lord Palmerston I could but remember how often I had heard father and Mr. S. exulting over his foreign dispatches by our own fireside. There were present, also, Lord John Russell, Mr. Gladstone, and Lord Granville. The latter we all thought very strikingly resembled in his appearance the poet Longfellow.

"After lunch the whole party ascended to the picture-gallery, passing on our way the grand staircase and hall, said to be the most magnificent in Europe. The company now began to assemble and throng the gallery, and very soon the vast room was crowded. Among the throng I remember many presentations, but of course must have forgotten many more. Archbishop Whately was there, with Mrs. and Miss Whately; Macaulay, with two of his sisters; Milman, the poet and historian; the Bishop of Oxford, Chevalier Bunsen and lady, and many more.

"When all the company were together, Lord Shaftesbury read a very short, kind, and considerate address in behalf of the women of England, expressive of their cordial welcome.

"This Stafford House meeting, in any view of it, is a most remarkable fact. Kind and gratifying as its arrangements have been to me, I am far from appropriating it to myself individually as a personal honor. I rather regard it as the most public expression possible of the feelings of the women of England on one of the most important questions of our day, that of individual liberty considered in its religious bearings."

What would the little station agent have thought could he have seen the erstwhile victim of his official contempt in these surroundings? When the reports of this Stafford House meeting reached America, Calhoun remarked that its chief significance lay in the fact that it would make abolitionism fashionable. A despised movement made fashionable by a little Yankee woman "just as thin and dry as a pinch of snuff."

After a partial rest in Paris, where she escaped publicity through some strategy, she went into Switzerland, where her presence became generally known in spite of precautions and she was hailed everywhere as *"Madame Besshare."* It was Scotland over again. All had read her book, and their enthusiasm seemed boundless. "Oh, Madame, do write another! Remember, our winter nights here are very long!" entreated the peasants in an Alpine village.

She finally returns to England, whence she writes as she leaves for home:" Thus, almost sadly, as a child might leave its home, I left the shores of kind, strong old England — the mother of us all."

She returns to America to be plunged into the thick of the Kansas and Nebraska struggle. She could think of nothing but slavery, and planned a story to be elaborated out of the material gathered in fashioning the "Key" for "Uncle Tom's Cabin." In her own words, the purpose of "Dred" is " to show the general effect of slavery on society; the various social disadvantages that it brings, even to its more favored advocates; the shiftlessness and misery, and backward tendency of all the economic arrange-

ments of slave states; the retrograding of good families into poverty; the deterioration of land; the worst demoralization of all classes, from the aristocratic tyrannical planter to the oppressed and poor white, which is the result of the introduction of slave labor." In "Dred" the didactic purpose is even more pronounced than in " Uncle Tom." Yet the book made a profound sensation in its day. Crossing again to England to secure a copyright, Mrs. Stowe wrote to her husband at Andover: " ' Dred' is selling over here wonderfully. Low says that, with all the means at his command, he has not been able to meet the demand. He sold fifty thousand in two weeks, and probably will sell as many more." And later she adds: "One hundred thousand copies of 'Dred' sold in four weeks! After that, who cares what critics say?... It goes everywhere, is read everywhere, and Mr. Low says that he puts the hundred and twenty-fifth thousand to press confidently. The fact that many good judges like it better than ' Uncle Tom ' is success enough!"

A little later she wrote from Paris: "It is wonderful that people here do not seem to get over *l* Uncle Tom ' a bit. The impression seems fresh as if just published. How often have they said, 'That book has revived the gospel among the poor of France; it has done more than all the books we have published put together. It has gone among *les ouvriers,* among the poor of Faubourg St. Antoine, and nobody knows how many have been led to Christ by it.' Is not this blessed, my dear husband? Is it not worth all the suffering of writing it?"

Mrs. Stowe returned from this second trip to Europe to meet the supreme sorrow of her life, — the death of her eldest son, Henry Stowe. One beautiful summer day in the year 1857, while swimming in the Connecticut River near Hanover, New Hampshire, where he was a student in Dartmouth College, he was seized with a cramp. He threw his arms about a classmate who tried to save him, and both sank together. As they rose to the surface, the friend cried out, "You 're drowning me, Henry!"

Immediately he relaxed his grasp, and sank to rise no more.

His mother was away on a visit when a telegram summoned her home. His classmates had just arrived with his body. As she looked upon his strong, peaceful young face, it was impossible for her to realize that her voice, which had ever had such power over him, could never now recall him. As she wrote to the Duchess of Sutherland, whom she and Henry had visited together only a few months before: "There had always been such union, such peculiar tenderness, between us. I had had such power always to call up answering feelings to my own, that it seemed impossible that he could be unmoved at my grief." No one had understood her as he had. No one had treated her with such constant and chivalrous tenderness. Her strange lapses of memory often excited outbursts of nervous irritability from other members of the family, but never from him. "A dreadful faintness of sorrow" came over her at times. As she went about the house, the pictures of which he was fond, the presents she had bought him, the photographs she was to show him, all pierced her heart. She writes that she would have been glad, "like the woman in the St. Bernard, to lie down with her arms around the wayside cross, and sleep away into a brighter scene."

"Henry's fair, sweet face looks down upon me now and then from out a cloud, and I feel again all the bitterness of the eternal 'No!' which says that I must never, never, in this life, see that face, and lean on that arm, hear that voice."

She wrote from Hanover, where she was visiting shortly after Henry's death: "A poor, deaf old slave woman, who has still five children in bondage, came to comfort me. 'Bear up, dear soul,' she said; 'you must bear it, for the Lord loves ye.'... She went on to say: 'Sunday is a heavy day to me, 'cause I can't work, an' I can't hear preachin', an' can't read, so I can't keep my mind off my poor children. Some on 'em the blessed Master's got, and they's safe; but oh, the 'er five I don't know where they are.'"

"What are our mother sorrows to this?" exclaims Mrs. Stowe. "I shall try to search out and redeem these children. ... Every sorrow I have, every lesson on the sacredness of family love, makes me the more determined to resist to the last this dreadful evil that makes so many mothers so much deeper mourners than I ever can be." So even in this supreme sorrow she seeks added strength for her warfare against the infliction of unnecessary suffering upon others.

On the completion of " The Minister's Wooing" in 1859 Professor and Mrs. Stowe returned to England for the third and last time. The whole family were abroad at this time except the youngest son Charley, then nine years old, to whom his father wrote the following graphic account of their experiences in England: "As it was court time. .. we wanted to go and see the court, so went over to St. George's Hall, a most magnificent structure, that beats the Boston State House all hollow, and Sir Robert Gerauld himself (the high sheriff of Lancashire) met us, and said he would get us a good place. So he took us away round a narrow, crooked passage, and opened a little door, where we saw nothing but a great, crimson curtain, which he told us to put aside and go straight on; and where do you think we all found ourselves? "Right on the platform with the judges in their big wigs and long robes, and facing the whole crowded court! It was enough to frighten a body into fits, but we took it quietly as we could, and your mamma looked as meek as Moses in her little, battered straw hat and gray cloak, seeming to say, 'I didn't come here o' purpose.'... Tuesday... we called at Stafford House, and enquired if the Duchess of Sutherland were there. A servant came out and said that the Duchess was in and would be very glad to see us; so your Mamma, Georgie, and I went walking up the magnificent staircase in the entrance hall, and the great, noble, brilliant Duchess came sailing down the stairs to meet us, in her white morning gown,... took your mamma into her great bosom, and folded her up till the little Yankee woman looked like a small

gray kitten half covered in a snowbank, and kissed and kissed her, and then she took up little Georgie and kissed her, and then she took my hand, and did n't kiss me.

"Next day we went to the Duchess's villa, near Windsor Castle, and had a grand time riding round the park, sailing on the Thames, and eating the very best dinner that was ever set on a table."

Professor and Mrs. Stowe's interest in things spiritual, keen as it had ever been, was greatly intensified by the death of their son, Henry. It took the form of a pathetic yet rational outreaching toward the future life, — a kind of calm but fervent protest against the eternal "No." In a letter written to her husband after he had returned home and she was in Italy, Mrs. Stowe says: "One thing I am convinced of,—that spiritualism is a reaction from the intense materialism of the present age. Luther, when he recognized a personal devil, was much nearer right. We ought to enter fully, at least, into the spiritualism of the Bible. Circles and spiritual jugglery I regard as the lying signs and wonders, with all deceivableness of unrighteousness; but there is a real spiritual spiritualism which has fallen into disuse, and must be revived, and there are, doubtless, people who, from constitutional formation, can more readily receive the impressions of the surrounding spiritual world. Such were apostles, prophets, and workers of miracles."

At this time Mrs. Stowe was not only acquainted with many of the eminent characters of Europe, but had among them a considerable number of real friends, of whom were the Ruskins, father and son, the Brownings, Mr. and Mrs. Lewes (George Eliot), Lady Byron, Mr. Low, her London publisher, the Duke and Duchess of Sutherland, the Duke and Duchess of Argyle, Lord Shaftesbury, Charles Kingsley, Lord Carlisle, who wrote the preface to the English edition of " Uncle Tom's Cabin," and Monsieur and Madame Belloc, he the Director of the French Academy of Design, and she the translator of "Uncle Tom's Cabin" into French.

In Mrs. Browning she found a particularly quick and ready response to her own feelings regarding things spiritual. In a letter written about a year after their friendship started, Mrs. Browning says: " Your letter, which would have given me pleasure if I had been in the midst of pleasures, came to me when little beside could have pleased. Dear friend, let me say it, I had had a great blow and loss in England, and you wrote things in that letter which seemed meant for me, meant to do me good, and which did me good, —the first good any letter or any talk did me; and it seems to me as strange, as more than a coincidence, that your first word since we parted in Rome last spring should have come to me in Rome, and bear so directly on an experience which you did not know of.

"... I don't know how people can keep up their prejudices against spiritualism with tears in their eyes, — how they are not, at least, thrown on the ' wish that it might be true,' and the investigation of the phenomena, by the abrupt shutting in their faces of the door of death, which shuts them out from the sight of their beloved. My tendency is to beat up against it like a crying child.

"... It ' De Profundis' refers to the greatest affliction of my life,—the only time when I felt *despair,*—written a year after or more. Forgive all these references. My husband calls me 'peculiar' in some things, — peculiarly *large,* perhaps. I can't articulate some names, or speak of certain afflictions;—no, not to him, — not after' all these years! It's a sort of dumbness of the soul. Blessed are those who can speak, I say. But don't you see from this how I must want 'spiritualism' above most persons?"

In a letter to George Eliot, Mrs. Stowe thus speaks of spiritualism: "I am perfectly aware of the frivolity and worthlessness of much of the revealings purporting to come from spirits. In my view, the worth or worthlessness of them has nothing to do with the question of fact.

"Do invisible spirits speak in anywise,—wise or foolish? — is the question a priori. I do not know of any reason why there should not be as many foolish virgins in the future state as in this. As I am a believer in the Bible and Christianity, I don't need these things as confirmations, and they are not likely to be a religion to me. I regard them simply as I do the phenomena of the Aurora Borealis, or Darwin's studies on natural selection, as curious studies into nature. Besides, I think some day we shall find a law by which all these facts will fall into their places...."

To this George Eliot replies: "... I desire on all subjects to keep an open mind... apart from personal contact with people who get money by public exhibitions as mediums, or with semi-idiots such as those who make a court for a Mrs., or other feminine personages of that kind, I would not willingly place any barriers between my mind and any possible channel of truth affecting the human lot." At about this period George Eliot writes Mrs. Stowe a letter in which she touches upon her own religious views in words which now appear startlingly prophetic. She says: "... Both traveling abroad and staying at home among our English sights and sports, one must continually feel how slowly the centuries work toward the moral good of men, and that thought lies very close to what you say you wonder concerning my religious point of view. I believe that religion, too, has to be modified according to the dominant phases; that a religion more perfect than any yet prevalent must express less care of personal consolation, and the more deeply awing sense of responsibility to man springing from sympathy with that which of all things is most certainly known to us, — the difficulty of the human lot. Letters are necessarily narrow and fragmentary, and, when one writes on wide subjects, are likely to create more misunderstanding than illumination. But I have little anxiety in writing to you, dear friend and fellow laborer; for you have had longer experience than I as a writer, and fuller experience as a woman, since you have borne children and known a mother's history from the beginning."

On the eve of her return to America for the third and last time, Mrs. Stowe received from John Ruskin this outburst of whimsical and affectionate pessimism,"... What a dreadful thing it is that people should have to go to America again, after coming to Europe! It seems to me an inversion of the order of nature. I think America is a sort of 'United States of Probation' out of which all wise people, being once delivered, and having obtained entrance into this better world, should never be expected to return (sentence irremediably ungrammatical), particularly when they have been making themselves cruelly pleasant to friends here.... I 've no heart to write about anything in Europe to you now. When are you coming back again? Please send me a line as soon as you get safe over, to say you are all — wrong, but not lost in the Atlantic." CHAPTER WI THROUGH SMOKE OF BATTLE

In June, 1860, just as Mrs. Stowe was on the eve of returning from Europe, she received the news of the death of Miss Annie Howard, the beautiful daughter of her intimate friend, Mrs. Tasker Howard. She had been almost as near and dear to Mrs. Stowe as an own daughter. To Mrs. Howard she writes: "Ah! Susie, I who have walked in this dark valley now for three years, what can I say to you who are entering it? One thing I can say — be not afraid and confounded if you find no apparent religious support at first." Her own heart, sore and bleeding from the loss of her son Henry, she had written to her husband: "Since I have been in Florence, I have been distressed by unutterable yearnings after him Henry, such sighings and outreachings, with a sense of utter darkness and separation." So she had moved in the midst of all the popularity and adulation that she received, with a hungry, aching heart. She wrote to her husband: "I long for my husband, my children, my room, my yard and garden and the beautiful trees of Andover."

The voyage home was as delightful as smooth seas and ac company could make it. Mrs. Stowe, Mr. and Mrs. Hawthorne, and Mr. and Mrs. James T. Fields made a rare assemblage of choice spirits. Hawthorne exclaimed one moonlight evening," 0, that we might never get there!" On the pier at East Boston, as the steamer docked, were Professor Stowe and Charley, adorned with smiles and cobwebs, — the latter acquired by poking their heads out of all sorts of unfrequented nooks and crannies in their efforts to get a first glimpse of the home-returning travelers.

The political horizon at this time was dark and threatening, but no one dreamed of what was coming or realized that the storm of war was about to break upon the nation. In a conversation at this time held in the Stone Cabin at Andover between Frederick Douglass, Mrs. Stowe, and an old colored woman, a kind of prophetess, called Sojourner Truth, Douglass, in all the bitterness of his soul, painted the hopelessness of the situation. What Mrs. Stowe said on the more hopeful side was swept away like a dam of rushes before the flood of his eloquence. Sojourner finally rose up to her majestic height and cried out, " Frederick! Frederick! Is God dead?" One evening, not long after, Professor Stowe and Doctor Lyman Beecher were talking over the situation which both admitted to be very dark indeed. They were sitting in rocking-chairs on opposite sides of the fire place. "Well, Father Beecher," exclaimed Professor Stowe, "there is one comfort! The Lord reigns!"

"Yes, Stowe," said the old man, making that characteristic gesture with his right fore-finger so well known to all who had heard him preach, "and the devil tries to, yes, the devil tries to!"

Never was there a more impressive scene in that old stone house in Andover than that which followed the receipt of the news of the attack on Fort Sumter. Twenty or thirty sturdy old farmers came to talk matters over with Professor Stowe, who was full of fight and courage. There was to be war he thought, but it would be short and decisive, and the Union would be saved. Neither Professor nor Mrs. Stowe ever had the least sympathy with Garrison's idea of secession. They often said that the Northern States were equally culpable with the Southern for the existence of slavery, and hence should not leave them MRS. STOWE, HENRY WARD

BEECHER. AND THEIR FATHER, DR. LY-MAN BEECHER alone to grapple unaided with dangers and difficulties which they had so largely helped to bring upon them. Mrs. Stowe asserted that the agitation kept up by the Anti-Slavery party in the United States, augmented by the general antipathy of Europe to slavery, had made unbearable the position of the slave-holding aristocracy. They felt themselves under the ban of the civilized world. "Two courses only were open to them," says Mrs. Stowe,—"to abandon slave institutions, the source of their wealth and political power, or to assert them with such an overwhelming force as to compel the respect and assent of mankind. They chose the latter."

She did not state, what was nevertheless the fact, that the strong sentiment in Europe against slavery was largely the result of "Uncle Tom's Cabin." The above quotation is taken from her reply to the "Address from the Women of England," published in the *Atlantic Monthly* in January, 1863. This address shows how clearly she grasped the situation. The thunder of the cannon in Charleston harbor spoke to her ears with no uncertain sound. The slave power had determined to sever a union they could no longer dominate. The address concludes: "The time of the Presidential canvass that elected Mr. Lincoln was the crisis of this great battle between slavery and freedom. The conflict had become narrowed down to the one point of the extension of slave territory. If the slave-holders could get states enough they could control and rule; if they were outnumbered by free states, their institutions by the very law of their nature would die of suffocation.... A President was elected pledged to opposition to this one thing alone (the extension of slavery) — a man known to be in favor of the Fugitive Slave Law, and other so-called compromises of the Constitution, but honest and faithful in his determination on this one subject. That this was indeed the vital point was shown by the result. The moment Lincoln's election was ascertained, the slave-holders resolved to destroy the Union they could no longer control."

Mrs. Stowe had herself contributed in a larger measure than she ever suspected to this situation. When Lincoln sent out his call for troops, thousands of young men responded whom "Uncle Tom's Cabin" had made the deadly enemies of slavery. One of the first to volunteer was her own son, the little boy who had cried out ten years before, when "Uncle Tom's Cabin" was read for the first time, "Oh, mama, slavery is the most cruel thing in the world!" The little boy of eleven was now a young man of twenty-one. He was at the time a student of medicine, studying under Dr. Oliver Wendell Holmes at the Harvard Medical School. Mrs. Stowe's son was full of the patriotic enthusiasm which filled the very air he breathed. He wished to enlist immediately. His mother wanted him to finish his studies and then enter the army as a surgeon. Dr. Holmes tried to persuade him to the same effect. One day when the three were arguing the matter in Dr. Holmes's study, throwing his hat on the floor with a dramatic gesture, the young man cried out hotly, "I should be ashamed to look my fellow men in the face if I did not enlist. People shall never say, 'Harriet Beecher Stowe's son is a coward.'"

There was no more resistance, and the next day he enlisted in Company A of the First Massachusetts Infantry. The young man felt very strongly that a son of the author of " Uncle Tom's Cabin" should be in the very front of the physical conflict which that book had done so much to precipitate. Mrs. Stowe was to learn from personal experience what thousands of mothers were feeling throughout the land. Immediately after the first battle of Bull Run a poor mother whose son had fallen in that action came a long distance to see Mrs. Stowe. "0, Mrs. Stowe, God only knows what I suffer," she said, the tears streaming down her wrinkled face, "but I wanted to see you and tell you about it," she continued, as she tightened her grasp on the hand that held hers. Mrs. Stowe, the tears rolling down her own cheeks, turned on the poor woman a face in which it seemed as if the sorrows of the nation were pictured in all their tragic

greatness and said, "Yes, you suffer, I suffer, we all suffer!" And she continued, " But we do not suffer alone. There is a Great Heart of Infinite Love that suffers with and for us!" The simple-hearted woman went away greatly comforted. Probably there arose in Mrs. Stowe's mind at that moment those prophetic words which she afterwards wrote: "It was God's will that this nation — the North as well as the South —should deeply and terribly suffer for the sin of consenting to and encouraging the great oppressions of the South; that the ill-gotten wealth, which had arisen from striking hands with oppression and robbery, should be paid back in the taxes of war; that the blood of the poor slave, that had cried so many years from the ground in vain, should be answered by the blood of the sons from the best hearthstones through all the free States; that the slave mothers, whose tears nobody regarded, should have with them a great company of weepers, North and South, — Rachel's weeping for their children and refusing to be comforted; that the free States that refused to listen when they were told of lingering starvation, cold, privation, and barbarous cruelty, as perpetrated on the slave, should have lingering starvation, cold, hunger, and cruelty doing its work among their own sons, at the hands of these slave-masters, with whose sins our nation had connived."

On June 11, 1861, she wrote to her husband from Brooklyn. "Yesterday noon Henry Ward Beecher came in, saying that the Commonwealth, with the First Massachusetts Regiment on board, had just sailed by.

"Immediately I was of course eager to get to Jersey City to see Fred. Sister Eunice said she would go with me, and in a few minutes she, Hattie, Sam Scoville, and I were in a carriage driving towards the Fulton Ferry. Upon reaching Jersey City we found that the boys were dining in the depot, an immense building with many tracks and platforms. It has a great cast-iron gallery just under the roof, apparently placed there with prophetic instinct of these times. There was a crowd of people pressing against the grated doors which were locked, but through which we could see the soldiers. It was with great difficulty that we were at last permitted to go inside, and that object seemed to be greatly aided by a bit of printed satin that some man gave Mr. Scoville.

"When we were in, a vast area of gray caps and blue overcoats was presented. The boys were eating, drinking, smoking, singing, and laughing. Company A was reported to be here, there, and everywhere. At last Sam spied Fred in the distance and went leaping across the tracks towards him. Immediately afterwards a blue-overcoated figure bristling with knapsack, and haversack, and looking like an assortment of packages, came rushing towards us.

"Fred was overjoyed you may be sure, and my first impulse was to wipe his face with my handkerchief before I kissed him. He was in high spirits in spite of the weight of blue overcoat, knapsack, etc., etc., that he would have formerly declared intolerable for half an hour.

"I gave him my handkerchief and Eunice gave him hers, with a sheer motherly instinct that is so strong within her, and then we filled his haversack with oranges.

"We stayed with Fred about two hours, during which time the gallery was filled with people cheering and waving their handkerchiefs. Every now and then the band played inspiring airs in which the soldiers joined with hearty voices. While some of the companies sang others were being drilled, and all seemed to be having a general jollification. The meal that had been provided was plentiful, and consisted of coffee, lemonade, sandwiches, etc.

"On our way out we were introduced to the Rev. Mr. Cudworth, chaplain of the regiment. He is a fine-looking man, with black hair and eyes set off by a white havelock. He wore a sword, and Fred touching it asked, 'Is this for use or ornament, sir?'

"' Let me see you in danger,' answered the chaplain, 'and you 'll find out.'

"I said to him I supposed he had had many entrusted to his kind offices, but I could not forbear adding one more to the number. He answered, 'You may rest assured, Mrs. Stowe, I will do all in my power.'

"We parted from Fred at the door. He said he felt lonesome enough Saturday evening on the Common in Boston, where everybody was taking leave of somebody, and he seemed to be the only one without a friend, but that this interview made up for it all.

"I saw also young Henry. Like Fred he is mysteriously changed, and wears an expression of gravity and care. So our boys come to manhood in a day. Now I am watching anxiously for the evening paper to tell me that the regiment has reached Washington in safety. "

Then came the news of the first battle of Bull Run. Again there was a long line of farmers' wagons drawn up before the Stone Cabin whose owners wanted to talk matters over with the Professor and his wife. Then came two lively letters from Fred Stowe written on the battlefield. The first day he did not get an opportunity to fire his gun at a real live"reb" all day, and the sun was, as he phrased it, " thundering hot." The shells, as they whizzed through the air, reminded him of great bumble-bees. For his part he had been neither hurt nor scared, and fired his gun only once, and that when he shot a young pig which they roasted on their bayonets and ate with great relish.

It is impossible for human beings to live all the time on a strain like a bow strung to its utmost tension. Not sombre gloom, but a cheerful excitement, pervaded the household in the old Stone Cabin at Andover most of the time during the War. Cheerfulness, hopefulness, and courage was indeed the atmosphere of Mrs. Stowe's life. She concluded a little speech at the celebration of her seventieth birthday with these words, "Let us never doubt. Everything that ought to happen is going to happen." This was her philosophy of life.

During the darkest days of the Civil War, when disaster and defeat to our armies in the field coupled with rumors of possible foreign intervention to compel the Northern States to recognize the Confederacy were filling the stoutest hearts with gloomy forebodings, Mrs. Stowe was talking one day with Dr. Holmes, in Mr. James T. Fields's study in Boston. She was speaking with unusual animation of her confidence that all would come out right in the end, and Dr. Holmes and Mr. Fields were listening intently. As she paused for a moment, Dr. Holmes eagerly exclaimed, "0, Mrs. Stowe, do go on! I do love to hear any one talk who believes so much more than I can!" It was about this time that her younger son went to his mother's room to bid her good-night and found her reading her New Testament, a candle in one hand, and in the other an iron crucifix that always hung over her bed. "What are you doing, mother?" he exclaimed in surprise. She looked up and said impressively, "My dear child, I am seeking the strength to bear what God has given us to bear in these sad days!"

"But why do you hold that crucifix in your hand?"

"Because it is a visible, tangible emblem of my Crucified Lord, and it helps me to cling to him! I want to feel that I hold fast to Him! That I have a dear friend to whom I can cling as well as a God to adore." The rest of the conversation was past repeating, but left an ineffaceable impression on her son's mind. Once when this same son rashly risked his life in skating over thin ice, his mother said to him as he was going to bed, "0, Charley boy, you 've kept the angels very busy to-day!" For Mrs. Stowe there was no natural and supernatural any more than to the writers of the New Testament. To her the supernatural was the habitual. It lay about us like a cloud, a world we might not see. "Our dead," she wrote, "are ministering angels: they teach us to love, they fill us with tenderness for all that can suffer."

In November, 1862, Mrs. Stowe, with many others, was invited to visit Washington, and attend a great Thanksgiving dinner which was to be provided for the thousands of fugitive slaves who had flocked to that city. This invitation she accepted the more gladly because her son's regiment was then encamped near the city. She wished also to have a talk with Mr. Lincoln. By a proclamation issued September 22, 1862, he had warned the states still in rebellion that unless they should return to their allegiance by January 1, 1863, he would, purely as a matter of military necessity, declare the slaves within their borders free. Mrs. Stowe was anxious to learn from his own lips what was to be his policy in this matter.

From Washington she writes to Professor Stowe in Andover: "Imagine a quiet little parlor with a bright coal fire, and the gaslight burning above the centre-table about which Hattie, Fred, and I are seated. Fred is as happy as happy can be with mother and sister once more. All day yesterday we spent in getting him. First we had to procure a permit to go to camp, then we went to the fort where the Colonel is, and then to another where the Brigadier-General is stationed. I was so afraid that they would not let him come with us, and was never happier than when at last he sprang into the carriage free to go with us for forty-eight hours. '0!' he exclaimed, in a sort of a rapture, 'this pays for a year and a half of fighting and hard work!'

"We tried hard to get the five o'clock train out to Laurel where James' James Beecher, her youngest brother regiment is stationed, as we wanted to spend Sunday all together; but could not catch it, and so had to content ourselves with what we could have. I have managed to secure a room for Fred next ours, and feel as if I had my boy at home once more. He is looking very well, and has grown in thickness, and is as loving and affectionate as a boy can be.

"I have just been writing a pathetic appeal to the Brigadier-General to let him stay with us for a week. I have also written to General Buckingham with regard to changing him from the infantry, in which there seems to be no prospect of anything but garrison duty, to the cavalry, which is full of constant activity.

"General B. called on us last evening.

He seemed to think that the prospect before us was, at best, of a long war. He was the officer deputed to carry the order to General McClellan relieving him of command of the army. He carried it to him in his tent about twelve o'clock at night. Burnside was there. McClellan said it was very unexpected, but immediately turned over the command. I said I thought he ought to have expected it after disregarding the President's order. General B. smiled, and said he supposed McClellan had done that so often before that he had no idea any notice would be taken of it this time."

On Thanksgiving Day, 1862, Mrs. Stowe attended the great dinner given to the Freedmen in Washington. In her reply to the " Address from the Women of England" sent to her so many years before, she thus alludes to this occasion: "This very day the writer of this reply has been present at a solemn religious festival in the national capital, given at the home of a portion of those fugitive slaves who have fled to our lines for protection, — who under the shadow of our flag find sympathy and succor. The national day of thanksgiving was there kept by over a thousand redeemed slaves, for whom Christian charity had spread an ample repast. Our sisters, we wish you could have witnessed the scene. We wish you could have heard the prayer of a blind old negro, called among his followers John the Baptist, when in touching, broken English he poured forth his thanksgiving. We wish you could have heard the sound of that strange rhythmical chant, which is now forbidden to be sung on Southern plantations, the psalm of this modern exodus, — which combines the barbaric fire of the 'Marseillaise' with the religious fervor of the old Hebrew prophet: — 'Oh, go down Moses,
Way down into Egypt's land!
Tell King Pharaoh
To let my people go!
    Stand away dere, Stand away dere,
And let my people go!'"

What impressed Mrs. Stowe most strongly was that the burden of this old negro's prayer was for humility. His great fear for himself and his people

seemed to be that, becoming filled with pride, they might forget the God who had saved them.

Mrs. Stowe, in telling of her interview with Lincoln at this time, dwelt particularly on the rustic pleasantry with which that great man received her. She was introduced into a cosy room where the President had been seated before an open fire, for the day was damp and chilly. It was Mr. Seward who introduced her, and Mr. Lincoln rose awkwardly from his chair, saying, "Why, Mrs. Stowe, right glad to see you!" Then with a humorous twinkle in his eye, he said, "So you 're the little woman who wrote the book that made this great war! Sit down, please," he added, as he seated himself once more before the fire, meditatively warming his immense hands over the smouldering embers by first extending the palms, and then turning his wrists so that the grateful warmth reached the backs of his hands. The first thing he said was, "I do love an open fire. I always had one to home." Mrs. Stowe particularly remarked on the expression "to home." "Mr. Lincoln," said Mrs. Stowe, "I want to ask you about your views on emancipation." It was on that subject that the conversation turned. Mrs. Stowe, like so many others at this time, had failed to grasp Lincoln's far-sighted statesmanship. "Mr. Lincoln has been too slow," she said, speaking of what she called his "Confiscation Bill." "He should have done it sooner, and with an impulse...." Bismarck has said something to the effect that a statesman who should permit himself to be guided exclusively by abstract moral considerations in his public acts would be like a man taking a long pole in his mouth and trying to run through a thick woods on a dark night. Would it have been for the best interests of humanity to have had a John Brown or a Garrison in Lincoln's place in those critical moments of the Civil War?

At this period Mrs. Stowe's interest in literature was overwhelmed by the intensity with which she entered into the great struggle that was going on about her. She wrote to the *Independent*, "The agitations and mental excitements of the war have in the case of the writer, as in the case of many others, used up the time and strength that would have been devoted to authorship.

"Who could write on stories that had a son to send to battle, with Washington beleaguered, and the whole country shaken as with an earthquake?"

Notwithstanding all this, " Agnes of Sorrento" and "The Pearl of Orr's Island" were finished during the darkest days of the Civil War. Not long after writing thus to the *Independent* Mrs. Stowe received the following letter: —

Gettysburg, Penn., Saturday, *July* 11, 9.30 P. M.

Mrs. H. B. Stowe:

Dear Madam, — Among the thousands of wounded and dying men on this war-scarred field, I have just met with your son, Captain Stowe. If you have not already heard from him, it may cheer your heart to know that he is in the hands of good kind friends. He was struck by a fragment of a shell which entered his right ear. He is quiet and cheerful, and longs to see some member of his family, and is, above all, anxious that they should hear from him as soon as possible. I assured him I would write at once, and though I am wearied by a week's labor here among scenes of terrible suffering, I know, that to a mother's anxious heart, even a hasty scrawl about her boy will be more than welcome.

May God bless and sustain you in this troubled time!

Yours with sincere sympathy,

J. M. Cromwell.

A similar letter came to Rev. Charles Beecher of Georgetown, Massachusetts, and he, together with Professor Stowe, started immediately for the battle-field. At Springfield, Massachusetts, Professor Stowe had all his money stolen, and returned to Andover in abject despair. In a few days, however, young Captain Stowe was stretched in the sun on the veranda of the old stone house, while his cousin, Lieutenant Fred Beecher, literally shot to pieces, lay on a couch in his father's home, fluttering between life and death. So were the stern realities of the war brought home to Mrs.

Stowe and her family circle.

Mrs. Stowe's most prominent public act during the Civil War was her reply to the "affectionate and Christian address to the women of America," which had been sent her immediately after the publication of " Uncle Tom's Cabin." It had been exhibited for the first time at the Boston Anti-Slavery Fair in 1853. It was in twenty-six stout folio volumes bound in morocco, an American eagle on the back of each, the address finely illuminated in vellum on the first page of the first volume, and contained nearly six thousand autograph signatures of Englishwomen of every rank and class, from the foot of the throne to the back-kitchen areas. It was an appeal to the women of America to use their utmost efforts to do away with slavery and all its horrors, immediately and forever! Considering the state of public feeling at the time, this remarkable document was hardly an olive-branch. While unquestionably prompted by the highest motives, its wisdom and timeliness were more than doubtful.

For nearly ten years it had slumbered in its solid oak case, unanswered, when on the twentyseventh day of November, 1862, Mrs. Stowe wrote her reply to which we have already frequently referred. Mrs. Stowe's motive in this reply was to enlist the sympathies of the English public on the side of the Northern States. It was the same motive that prompted her brother, Henry Ward Beecher, to undertake his mission to England. This purpose she herself explains in these few vigorous sentences: "It became important for the new Confederation to secure the assistance of foreign powers, and infinite pains were then taken to blind and bewilder the mind of England as to the real issue of the conflict in America.

"It has been often and earnestly asserted that slavery had nothing to do with this conflict; that it was a mere struggle for power; that the only object was to restore the Union as it was, with all its abuses. It is to be admitted that expressions have proceeded from the national administration which naturally gave rise to misapprehension, and therefore we beg to speak to you on this subject more fully."

Mrs. Stowe did not write this reply until she had had the personal interview with Mr. Lincoln already described, and had learned from the President himself the policy of his administration regarding slavery, — notably his little understood Border-State policy. Not till then did she break the silence she had maintained for nearly ten years. She did not reply sooner because she felt that any reply that she might write would, in the existing state of public feeling, do far more harm than good. She waited until the time was ripe, and then struck effectively. "In the beginning of the struggle," she writes, " the voices that reached us across the water said, 'If we were only sure you were fighting for the abolition of slavery, we should not dare to say whither our sympathies for your cause might not carry us.' Such, as we heard, were the words of the honored and religious nobleman Lord Shaftesbury who drafted this very letter you signed, and sent us, and to which we are now replying.

"When these words reached us, we said, 'We can wait, our friends in England will soon see whither this conflict is tending.' A year and a half have passed, step after step has been taken for liberty; chain after chain has fallen, till the march of our armies is choked and clogged by the glad flocking of emancipated slaves; the day of final emancipation is set; the Border States begin to move in voluntary assent. Here we see plainly traces of her interview with Lincoln. It was he who called her attention to the gradual change of sentiment in the Border States that had made the Emancipation Proclamation possible and expedient. Universal freedom for all dawns like the sun in the distant horizon, and still no voice from England. No voice? Yes, we have heard on the high seas the voice of a war-steamer, built for a man-stealing Confederacy, with English gold, in an English dockyard, going out of an English harbor, manned by English sailors, with the full knowledge of English government officers, in defiance of the Queen's proclamation of neutrality! So far has English sympathy overflowed! We have heard of other steamers, iron-clad, designed to furnish to a slavery-defending Confederacy its only lack, — a navy for the high seas. We have heard that the British Evangelical Alliance refuses to express sympathy with the liberating party when requested to do so by the French Evangelical Alliance. We find in the English newspapers all those sad degrees in the downward sliding scale of defending and apologizing for slave-holders and slave-holding, with which we have so many years contended in our own country. We find the President's Proclamation of Emancipation spoken of in those papers only as an incitement to servile insurrection. Nay, more, — we find in your papers from thoughtful men the admission of the rapid decline of Anti-Slavery sentiments in England."

This reply produced a profound sensation in England, and did much to prevent armed intervention in behalf of the Confederacy. John Bright wrote to Mrs. Stowe: "I read every word of it the reply) with intense interest, and am quite sure that its effect upon public opinion here has been marked and beneficial. It has covered some with shame, and it has compelled many to think, and it has stimulated not a few to act. Before this reaches you, you will have seen what large and earnest meetings have been held in all our towns in favor of Abolition, and the North. No town has a building large enough to contain those who come to listen, to applaud, and to vote in favor of freedom and the Union. The effect of this is evident on our newspapers and on the tone of Parliament, where now nobody says a word in favor of recognition or mediation, or any such thing." This letter, written on the 9th of March, 1863, before the battle of Gettysburg, shows that Mrs. Stowe's "reply" was one of the great influences that changed the sentiment of the English people towards the Confederacy.

On January 1,1863, in the terms of his announcement previously made, Lincoln issued the Emancipation Proclamation. Mrs. Stowe was at a concert in the Music Hall when the news reached Boston and was announced from the stage to the immense audience. During the wild demonstrations of enthusiasm which followed some one in the audience called attention to Mrs. Stowe's presence in the gallery. Instantly the multitude turned their faces upwards hers, waving their handkerchiefs and smiling. Her face all aglow with pleasure and excitement, she rose and bowed to right and left. It was a moment of triumph, — the crowning of a life's work.

That Lincoln had been none too deliberate in issuing this proclamation was abundantly proved by the falling off in the Republican vote which was its immediate though temporary effect. Of course it did not apply to slave states not in rebellion, nor to those that had been conquered. The real work was to be accomplished by the constitutional amendment passed later. It virtually marked, however, the end of slavery in the United States, and so did away with the underlying cause of the Civil War. For no one can deny had there been no slavery there would have been no servicession and no war.

It was during this dark period of the war that Mrs. Stowe moved from Andover to Hartford, Connecticut. In a grove of oaks on the bank of a little river she built a large and expensive house, far better planned for the climate of Florida than Connecticut. The spot had been one of her favorite resorts as a schoolgirl. Here she had dreamed away many a summer and autumn day with Georgiana May or Catherine Cogswell. She had often whimsically assured these friends that here would she build a house when she was rich. She purchased the land with part of the proceeds of the first sale of "Uncle Tom's Cabin." The house was finished largely in the natural wood from the oaks and chestnuts cut on the place. The whole enterprise, an effort to realize a girlhood dream, took time, strength, and money far beyond her resources. It was a hungry octopus that nearly sucked the life blood out of the brave little woman. From Professor Stowe she could expect no aid, as he was the most helpless and unpractical of men; and little sympathy, as the whole undertaking was contrary to his best judgment and repeated warnings. Gloomy prognostications of disaster were his only contributions to a solution of the difficult situation. In the mean time, as the spider spins its home out of its own vitals, so Mrs. Stowe spun her way out of her pecuniary troubles by the creations of her own brain. Then her son came home from the war with broken body and shattered will. What to do for him was a perplexing problem. Had it not been for the kind helpfulness of her sister Mary and her big-hearted husband, Mr. Thomas Perkins, a leading lawyer of Hartford, Mrs. Stowe must have sunk into her grave under the burdens that crushed down upon her at this time. Yet these burdens she had largely brought upon herself. With all her power and sound sense she was a dreamer of dreams. Her ideas of finance might work among angels, but they were not adapted to New England. She believed in everybody and trusted everybody, and was cheated and imposed upon without let or hindrance.

She wrote, at this time, to her publisher, Mr. Fields: " Can I tell you what it is to begin to keep house in an unfinished home and place, dependent on a carpenter, a plumber, a mason, a bell-hanger, who come and go at their own sweet will, breaking in, making all sorts of dust, chips, dirt, going off in the midst leaving all standing, — reappearing at uncertain intervals making more dust, chips, and dirt? One parlor and my library have thus risen piecemeal by disturbance and convulsions. They are almost done now, and the last box of books is almost unpacked, but my head aches so with the past confusion that I cannot get up any feeling of rest. I can't enjoy,—can't feel a minute to sit down and say 'it is done.'"

Then again she writes, speaking of her daughter's coming marriage: "I am in trouble, — have been in trouble ever since my turtledoves announced their intention of pairing in June instead of August, because it entailed on me an immediate necessity of bringing everything, out of doors and in, to a state of completeness for the wedding exhibition in June. The garden must be planted, the lawn graded, harrowed, rolled, seeded, and the grass got up and growing, stumps got out and shrubs and trees got in, conservatory made over, beds planted, holes filled, — and all by three very slippery sort of Irishmen, who had at any time rather be minding their own business than mine. I have back doorsteps to be made, and troughs, screens, and what not; papering, painting, varnishing hitherto neglected, to be completed; also spring house-cleaning, also dress-making for one bride and three ordinary females, also and and 's wardrobes to be overlooked, carpets to be made and put down; also a revolution in the kitchen cabinet, threatening for a time to blow up the whole establishment altogether." It is needless to say that authorship under such conditions would appear to be a sheer impossibility. It would have been to any one but Mrs. Stowe.

The house was a most delightful one for summer, but when the severe cold of winter came it was impossible with any expenditure for fuel to heat it properly. Water pipes were continually freezing and bursting, so that the establishment proved an annuity to the fortunate plumber, who, with an eye to future business, had arranged a complicated system that kept more than one man busy during the entire season. The Professor was submerged in waves and billows of the blues, and made daily predictions that the whole family would end in the poorhouse. One day, in a spasm of economy, he attempted to mend personally a broken pane of glass in one of the cellar windows with a sheet of tin, two shingle nails, and a tackhammer. After breaking out all the remaining glass in the sash, he went to his room in an agony of despair, while Mrs. Stowe quietly sent for a glazier to attend to the matter properly. In all matters pertaining to literature and scholarship he was a ready help in every time of need, but the problem of taking care of a great house with extensive grounds on inadequate means kept him palpitating with anxiety and woe.

Every one thought Mrs. Stowe had made a fortune out of her books, and all were piously resolved to relieve her of the dangers and temptations of great wealth so far as lay in their power. Although she received large sums from her publishers, all was swallowed up by the octopus on the river-side; that is, by architect, builder, carpenters, and plumbers. They had good digestions and swallowed her dollars as fast as she could feed them to them.

CHAPTER VIII LIFE IN THE SOUTH
In 1865 Mrs. Stowe's son, Captain Stowe, resigned his commission in the army, and attempted to resume his medical studies. This, however, proved impossible. From time to time the pain of the wound received at Gettysburg drove him to the verge of insanity. In such a state continuous mental application was out of the question. Just at this time a number of Connecticut people, retired army officers among them, had taken an old cotton plantation in Florida to raise cotton by free labor. Mrs. Stowe was enthusiastic over the scheme! Here was not only a solution of her perplexity with regard to her son, but a mission! She was always looking for a mission. It was a necessity of her mind to persuade herself that some higher end was being sought in everything she did from raising potatoes to writing a book. Consequently, she put money into the project that she could ill afford to lose. Naturally enough the whole thing was a failure, and practically amounted to maintaining a free boarding house for a year or more for a gang of lazy negroes. What cotton was raised cost more than it could have been sold for; and, as a matter of fact, it was never sold, because what was not ruined by mildew was eaten by army worms. In this enterprise Mrs. Stowe lost in the neighborhood of ten thousand dollars. She apparently felt little or no regret for the pecuniary loss. So much good had been done among the negroes by the preaching, praying, and hymn singingGer many souls had probably been saved, and if so what was the loss of ten thousand dollars compared with such a gain!

About this time Captain Stowe rowed across the St. Johns River on a fishing excursion and discovered Mandarin Cove and a snug little orange grove that the owner was anxious to sell for a reasonable price. Here was a new possibility! If he could not raise cotton, he could at least raise oranges, and there seemed a fair prospect of a good profit in the enterprise.

It was impossible, however, for his mother to take a merely commercial view of any undertaking. She immediately turned her mind to the possibilities of doing good that were connected with the scheme. She writes to her brother, the Rev. Charles Beecher of Georgetown, Massachusetts, as follows: "My plan of going to Florida, as it lies in my mind, is not in any sense a mere worldly enterprise. I have for many years had a longing to be more immediately doing Christ's work on earth. My heart is with that poor people whose cause in words I have tried to plead, and who, now ignorant and docile, are just in that formative stage in which, whoever seizes, has them.

"Corrupt politicians are already beginning to speculate on them as possible capital for their schemes, and fill their poor heads with all sorts of vagaries. Florida is the state into which they have, more than anywhere else, been pouring. Emigration is positively and decidedly setting that way; but as yet it is mere worldly emigration, with the hope of making money, nothing more.

"The Episcopal Church is, however, undertaking, under direction of the future Bishop of Florida, a wide embracing scheme of Christian activity for the whole state. In this work I desire to be associated, and my plan is to locate at some salient point on the St. Johns River, where I can form the nucleus of a Christian neighborhood whose influence shall be felt far beyond its own limits."

About a year later she writes him: "We are now thinking of a place in Mandarin much more beautiful than any other in the vicinity. It has on it five large date palms, an olive tree in full bearing, besides a fine orange grove that this year will yield about seventy-five thousand oranges. If we get that, then, I want you to consider the expediency of buying the one next to it. It contains about two hundred acres of land, on which is a fine orange grove, the fruit of which last year brought in two thousand dollars as sold at the wharf.

"It is right on the river, and four steamers pass it each week on their way to Savannah and Charleston. There is on the place a very comfortable cottage, as houses go out there, where they do not need to be built as substantially as with us.

"I am now in correspondence with the Bishop of Florida, with a view to establishing a line of churches along the St. Johns River, and if I settle at Mandarin it will be one of my stations. Will you consent to enter the Episcopal Church and be our clergyman? You are just the man we want! If my tastes and feelings did not incline me towards the Church, I should still choose it as the best system for training immature minds such as those of our negroes. The system was composed with reference to the wants of the laboring class of England at a time when they were as ignorant as our negroes now are.

"I long to be at this work and cannot think of it without my heart burning within me. Still I leave all with my God, and only hope He will open the way for me to do all that I want to for this poor people."

Mrs. Stowe bought the place, and in one of her letters to George Eliot thus describes how the home was established: "The history of the cottage is this: I found a hut built close to a great live-oak twenty-five feet in girth, and with overarching boughs eighty feet up in the air, spreading like a firmament, and all swaying with mossy festoons. We began to live here, and gradually we improved the hut by lath, plaster, and paper. Then we threw out a wide veranda all around, for in these regions the veranda is the living room of the house. Ours had to be built around the trunk of the tree, so that our cottage has a peculiar and original air, and seems as if it were half tree, or something that has grown out of the tree. We added

on parts, and have thrown out gables and chambers, as a tree throws out new branches, till our cottage is like nobody's else, and yet we settle into it with real enjoyment. There are all sorts of queer little rooms in it, and we are at present accommodating a family of seventeen souls. In front, the beautiful, grand St. Johns River stretches five miles from shore to shore, and we watch the steamboats plying back and forth to the great world we are out of. On all sides large orange trees, with their dense shade, and ever-vivid green, shut out the broiling sun so that we can sit, and walk, and live in the open air. Our winter here is only cool, bracing, outdoor weather without snow. No month without flowers blooming in the open air and lettuce and peas growing in the garden. The summer range is about 90, but the sea breezes keep the air delightfully cool.

"Though resembling Italy in climate Florida is wholly different in the appearance of nature,—the plants, the birds, the animals, are all different. The green tidiness of England here gives way to a wild and rugged savageness of beauty. Every tree bursts forth with flowers; wild vines and creepers execute delirious gambols, and weave and interweave in interminable labyrinths. Yet here, in the great sandy plains back of our house, there is a constant wondering sense of beauty in the wild wonderful growths of nature. First of all the pines—high as the stone pines of Italy — with long leaves, eighteen inches long, through which there is a constant dreamy sound as if of dashing waters. Then the live-oaks, and the water-oaks, narrow-leaved evergreens, which grow to enormous size, and whose branches are draped with long festoons of the gray moss. There is a great wild park of these trees back of us, which, with the dazzling varnished green of the new spring leaves and the swaying drapery of moss, looks like a sort of enchanted grotto. Underneath grow up lilies and ornamental flowering shrubs, and the yellow jessamine climbs up into and over everything with fragrant golden bells and buds. This wild, wonderful,

bright, and vivid growth, that is all new, strange, and unknown by name to me, has a charm for me. It is the place to forget the outside world and live in one's self.

"We emigrate in solid family: my two dear daughters, husband, self, and servants come together to spend the winter here, and so together to our Northern home in summer. My twin daughters relieve me from all domestic care; they are lively, vivacious, with a real genius for practical life. We have around us a little settlement of neighbors, who, like ourselves, have a winter home here, and live an easy, undress, picnic kind of a life far from the world and its cares.

"When I get here I enter another life. The world recedes; I am out of it; it ceases to influence; its bustle and noise die away in the far distance, and here is no winter; an open-air life, — a quaint, rude, wild wilderness life, both rude and rich, but when I am here I write more letters to friends than I do elsewhere. The mail comes only twice a week and is a great event. My old rabbi and I here set up our tent, he with German and Greek and Hebrew, devouring all sorts of blackletter books, and I spinning ideal webs out of bits he lets fall here and there."

But with all this enjoyment of the material world, with its tangible realities, the spiritual aim was not forgotten. She carried out her desire to "form the nucleus of a Christian neighborhood whose influence shall be felt far beyond its own limits." With her own money she built a little church and schoolhouse, where for many years Professor Stowe preached earnest, eloquent sermons, and she taught a Sunday-school class of colored children. In a letter written to her son in 1875, she gives the following picture of an Easter Sunday in the little church and schoolhouse: —

"It was the week before Easter, and we had on our minds the dressing of the church. There were my two Gothic fireboards to be turned into a pulpit for the occasion. I went to Jacksonville and got a five-inch moulding for a base, and then had one fireboard sawed in two, so that there was an arched panel for each end. Then came a rummage for something for a top, and to make a desk of, until it suddenly occurred to me that our old black walnut extension table had a set of leaves. They were exactly the thing. The whole was trimmed with a beading of yellow pine, and rubbed, and pumice-stoned, and oiled, and I got out my tubes of paint and painted the nail holes with Vandyke brown. By Saturday morning it was a lovely little Gothic pulpit, and Anthony took it over to the schoolhouse and took away the old desk which I gave him for his meeting-house.

"That afternoon we drove into the woods and gathered a quantity of superb Easter lilies, pawpaw, sparkleberry, great fern leaves, and cedar. In the evening the girls went over to the Meads to practice Easter hymns; but I sat at home and made a cross eighteen inches long of cedar and white lilies. This Southern cedar is the most exquisite thing, — it is so feathery and delicate.

"Sunday morning was cool and bright, a most perfect Easter. Our little church was full, and everybody seemed delighted with the decorations. Mr. Stowe preached a sermon to show that Christ is going to put everything right at last, which is comforting. So the day was one of real pleasure, and also I trust of real benefit, to the poor souls who learned from it that Christ is indeed risen for them."

It was a number of years before Mrs. Stowe was able to carry out her original plan of establishing an Episcopal church in Mandarin. It was not till 1884 that she writes, "Mandarin looks very gay and airy now with its new villas, and our new church and rectory. Our minister is perfect. I wish you could know him. He wants only physical strength. In everything else he is all one could ask."

Nothing delighted Mrs. Stowe more than the growing prosperity of the colored people. It was this that she emphasized in her little talk at the celebration of her seventieth birthday, when she said: —

"... If any one of you have doubt, or sorrow, or pain, if you doubt about this world, just remember what God has done; just remember that this great sorrow of slavery has gone, has gone forever. I see it every day at the South. I walk about there and see the lowly cabins. I see these people growing richer and richer. I see men very happy in their lowly lot; but, to be sure, you must have patience with them. They are not perfect, but have their faults, and they are serious faults in the view of white people. But they are very happy, that is evident, and they do know how to enjoy themselves, — a great deal more than you do. An old negro friend in our neighborhood has got a new, nice two-story house, and an orange grove, and a sugar mill. He has got a lot of money besides. Mr. Stowe met him one day, and he said, 'I've got twenty head of cattle, four head of "hoss," forty head of hen, and I have got ten children, *all mine, every one mine!'* Well, now, that's a thing that a black man could not say once, and this man was sixty years old before he could say it. With all the faults of the colored people, take a man of sixty and put him down with nothing but his hands, how many could say as much as that? I think they have done well. A little while ago they had an evening festival at his house and raised fifty dollars. We white folks took our carriages, and when we reached the house we found it fixed nicely. Every one of his daughters knew how to cook. They had a good place for the festival. Their suppers were spread on little white tables with nice clean cloths on them. People paid fifty cents for supper. They got between fifty and sixty dollars, and had one of the best frolics you could imagine. They had also for supper ice cream that they made for themselves. That's the sort of thing I see going on around me." And then she concludes with the words already quoted, "Let us never doubt. Everything that ought to happen is going to happen."

Mrs. Stowe first visited Mandarin in 1866. She and her youngest son made the journey by way of Washington, and thence by steamboat to Aqua Creek, and from there to Charleston, South Carolina, by a special military train. On their arrival at Charleston, a Southern gentleman called upon them; and introducing himself as a former major in the Confederate army, explained that his mother and sisters were anxious to entertain them at their home, because of what they owed to Mrs. Stowe's nephew, Colonel Robert Beecher, for the way in which he had protected them from the brutality of some Northern soldiers when they were defenseless in their home during the burning of Columbia. When the three ladies were alone and unprotected in the burning city, a mob of half-drunken soldiers broke into their house. One of the daughters was seriously ill, and her mother feared that the shock and fright might kill her. Seeing an officer passing the house in the uniform of a Federal Colonel, she rushed to the door and begged him for protection. With drawn sword and revolver, Colonel Beecher drove the drunken soldiers from the house, and while the Union army remained in Columbia he was both the guest and the protector of this family. Mrs. Stowe's son has never forgotten a letter he saw while he and his mother were enjoying the ideal hospitality of this family, — a letter written on the battle-field by a dying soldier to his mother. The young man had joined the Confederate army as he was about to enter the Presbyterian ministry, and he bravely faced death with as much confidence that he was fighting for righteousness as ever inspired a crusader. The whole tone of his letter breathed satisfaction that he had been permitted to lay down his life for the cause of God and truth as against injustice and oppression. Even the Greek mind never conceived a tragedy more terrible than the war between the states in North America.

From Charleston they proceeded to Mandarin by the steamer Dictator, commanded by Captain Atkins, who had been a blockade runner during the war. He was a brisk little man, with a very red face and bristling whiskers, who showed an almost pathetic solicitude for Mrs. Stowe's comfort and safety. One fair Sunday afternoon the Dictator sailed majestically into Mandarin Cove, and landed them within a stone's throw of the Stowe cottage. Here at Mandarin Professor Stowe, ably seconded by Mrs. Stowe, acted as a pastor to the whole neighborhood, both white and black. There was not a secluded nook on the river bank, or a lonely hut in the pine woods, that they did not visit together, jolting over roots and stumps and laboring through the sand, seated in camp chairs in a rude, two-wheeled cart drawn by Fly, a meditative and philosophical mule. As Mrs. Stowe writes: "You ought to see us riding out in our mule cart. Poor fly, the last of pea time, who looks like an animated hair trunk, and the wagon and harness to match! It is too funny; but we enjoy it hugely!" The big, corpulent, gray-bearded Professor, with his gold spectacles and broad-brimmed Quaker hat, and his thin little wife, dreamy and abstracted, with her shabby dress and old straw bonnet all awry, gazing up into the pine trees and singing in utter self-forgetfulness as they jolted along: —

"' We 're on our journey home

Where Christ our Lord has gone,' " etc., made a picture both amusing and appealing.

Way back in the woods in a barren clearing among the whispering trees was a little Roman Catholic church, blistering in the tropical sun. Adjoining it was a nunnery where lived three French Sisters of the Church. Near by in a little hut lived an Italian priest, Father Batazzi. If ever the spirit of the Christ dwelt in human souls, it dwelt in these self-sacrificing representatives of the Roman Catholic Church. Once or twice a month Fly was harnessed into the mule cart, and the Professor and his wife started with baskets of oranges and packages of all sorts of creature-comforts to visit Father Batazzi and the Sisters. When they met there was no Catholic or Protestant, but an absolute oneness of spirit. The Professor in his bluff, hearty way, always suggested that these visits be closed with prayer. The good priest and the Sisters made no objection, Father Batazzi frequently joining in in his broken English.

The priest started a little vineyard in the dreary pine waste, which greatly cheered his heart. It was like a bit of his own beloved Italy in this far-off land. But one night some of those Florida cows, which might well serve as prototypes of the lean kine that King Pharaoh saw in his troubled dreams, broke into the inclosure and ate up all the vines. "Oh, Father Batazzi," exclaimed Mrs. Stowe a day or two afterwards, "what a perfect shame that those wretched cows ate your vines!"

"Oh no, Mrs. Stowe, dat iz all right! It vas gut for ze cows, and it vas gut for me! I fear zat I have made an iddel of dose vines!"

When the terrible scourge of yellow fever broke out in Fernandina, and people forsook their dead and their dying to flee in blind and unpitying terror, Father Batazzi and the Sisters went to the plague-stricken city, nursed the sick, cared for the dying, and buried the dead. In this noble service one of the Sisters laid down her life.

One day the Professor and his wife went on foot on some charitable errand. Returning they completely lost their way in the delirious labyrinth of a live-oak hummock. Mrs. Stowe lost her eye-glasses, and the Professor's spectacles were snatched from his nose by a malicious creeping vine. It was growing late and the light was waning. The Professor, availing himself of his mighty vocal powers, set up a stentorian shouting. Anthony, their negro man, who was on his way home, was drawn to the spot by the alarming uproar. He was a preacher with native and timely eloquence. Peering at them through the gloom, he sang out," Well, well, is dat you? Why you dun gone got loss, eh? jah! jah! I will proceed to lead you out by a more delectable way dan dat by which you entered dis ar thicket!"

Although very proud of his wife and her reputation, nevertheless it was galling to Mr. Stowe at times to be set completely in the shade by his more distinguished wife. On one occasionalady remarked to him, "I am delighted to meet you, Professor Stowe, but I must confess I should have preferred to have met Mrs. Stowe!"

"So had I, madam!" was the prompt and significant retort.

An enterprising steamboat company in Jacksonville advertised excursions to Mandarin and Mrs. Stowe's orange grove, — so much for the round trip, — without consulting her, or offering her consideration of any sort for being made a public spectacle. The Professor and his wife took it, however, very good-naturedly, and received those who came with a courteous hospitality. For the most part these persons were well behaved, and to one who enjoyed sociability as heartily as did Professor Stowe the experience had its pleasant side. One day, however, a man broke off a branch of an orange tree directly under the Professor's eyes. On Mr. Stowe's addressing him in vigorous language, he timidly replied, "Why, I thought this was Mrs. Stowe's place!"

"I would have you understand, sir!" thundered the Professor, " that I am the proprietor and protector both of Mrs. Stowe and this place!"

While at Mandarin Mrs. Stowe made many excursions to various parts of the state, and was everywhere treated with cordial and courteous hospitality. On one of these trips a Southern woman was heard to say, "I am sure that I have been told that Mrs. Stowe is sorry that she wrote 'Uncle Tom's Cabin.' She is a good, kind-hearted woman, and I believe she would have cut off her right hand rather than write that book, if she could have foreseen all the misery she was to cause by it." After visiting her brother, the Rev. Charles Beecher, at Newport, Florida, she continued her journey to New Orleans, meeting with nothing but kindness and cordiality from the best class of Southern people. Both at Tallahassee and New Orleans she was warmly welcomed and tendered public receptions, given to show that there was no bitterness towards her personally. Throughout the journeys the colored people thronged the railroad stations to catch a glimpse of her as she was whirled by.

No words can better describe her life in Mandarin than these, "She went about doing good." This incident is in point. There came to Mandarin a gentleman who was suffering agonies from rheumatism. From very early life he had been bitterly prejudiced against" Churchianity." He denounced the churches, and all professing Christians as knaves and hypocrites. His natural asperities of temper had not been softened by his sufferings. His language and manners were far from engaging, and he was not popular. Mrs. Stowe made her observations on the man, and quietly managed to drop in upon him almost daily to tell him a bit of news or a funny story. Never a word, however, about the Church, the Bible, or Christians, and if he blazed out on these subjects she seemed dreamy and abstracted till he had cooled off. To the amazement of his family, he handed her one day two crisp twenty-dollar bills, and said, "I want you to let me have a little share in what you are doing in your church and Sunday-school, Mrs. Stowe. I don't make any professions of any kind, but I know a good thing when I see it!" She took the money with a quiet smile, but said little. She was not surprised because she believed in people. Just as the sun shines on the frozen ground and says, "You are not frozen ground, but a garden, soft and warm, and full of flowers," and lo! it is so, so she kindled the best in people.

It was a great grief to her when this little church and schoolhouse burned down, as it did one windy night. She says: " But to think of our church and schoolhouse being burned down just as we are ready to do something with it. I feel it most for the colored people, who were so anxious to have their school, and now have no place to have it in. We are all trying to raise what we can for a new building, and intend to get it up by March. If I were North now I would try giving some readings for this, and perhaps raise something."

There can be no doubt that the quiet Florida days prolonged for many years Mrs. Stowe's life and usefulness. Yet even this Patmos was not all rest for her. Financial difficulties still troubled and beset her.

"On gold depends, to gold still tends; All, all, alas we poor!"

Why should she have been poor when she wrote such popular books that brought her such handsome returns? Her publishers were liberal, even generous. She received ten thousand dollars for "Oldtown Folks," mostly in prepayments. Professor Stowe received ten thousand dollars in royalties for his book on the Bible, — a most remarkable record for a book of that nature. Yet they were, as the Professor said, "always plagued and poor!" We find Mrs. Stowe doing hack work like the editorship of a book entitled "The Men of Our Times." Fly and the mule cart could hardly be called family extravagances. No one who ever saw the Professor, his wife, or any of the family could suspect them of being unduly in bondage to the pomp and vanities of this world. As the Professor and his wife advanced in years there developed certain startling eccentricities in their mode of dress, but never any extravagances. To explain their chronic poverty is, however, not difficult.

In the first place they were lamentably deficient in that " root of all evil, the love of money." That is a Beecher failing from the old Doctor Lyman down. Henry Ward Beecher was as deficient in this way as his sister Harriet. He said, "Money is like gunpowder. It's no use except you fire it off!" As for old Lyman Beecher, when the ladies of his Boston church gave him fifty dollars to buy anew overcoat, he ran round the corner and popped it all into a missionary collection. His children were all like him. Thomas K. Beecher, when his Elmyra church tried to give him an annuity, said that "he'd take to the woods if they did, and that it was the ambition of his life to be a worthy object of charity in his old age." One might as well give money to a resurrection angel as to a genuine Beecher, and Mrs. Stowe was a Beecher, and very genuine. As to Professor Stowe, he was as like to her as like could be in this respect. He was descended from John Stow, the chronicler of London, to whom James I gave letters patent to solicit the alms of the good people of London because he had spent a life of unrequited service in collecting the historical monuments of England. Stow collected seven shillings and a sixpence, and the letters patent were extended for another twelvemonth. As a money-getter, his descendant was little more successful.

First, there was an open-handed generosity that gave without stint in private and public charities of every description. Then, there was an unsuspecting trustfulness in those who were ever eager to invest their money for them. As Mrs. Fields says in the "Life and Letters" Mrs. Stowe writes to Mr. Howard, "I have invested thirty-four thousand dollars in various ways, none of which can give me any immediate income." The probability is that these particular investments never gave her any income. It had been far better if she had spent it and got some satisfaction out of it. "My investment in this Southern place," she writes again, "is still one whose returns are in the future." That future never came. The orange grove was ruined by frosts and sold for a song! The enterprise of founding the "Christian Union" cost her and her brother, Henry Ward Beecher, thousands of dollars and never brought them a cent in return. So her money vanished like the morning cloud and the early dew, and she slaved at her pen far into old age. In 1872 she lost her truest friend and safest business adviser, Mr. Thomas C. Perkins, the husband of her sister Mary. She writes: "The blow has fallen! My dear brother has left us! Nowhere in the world had I a truer friend. It is a blow that strikes deep on my life and makes me feel that it is like ice breaking under my feet. Those who truly love us, and on whom we may at all times depend, are not many, and all my life he has been one of these."

It is little that she did not have money, or the faculty for getting and keeping it. She had wealth far more satisfactory and abiding. "Sometimes in my sleep I have such nearness to the blessed, it is almost as if one voice after another whispers to me,' Thou shalt tread upon the lion and the adder.' 'The eternal God is thy refuge, and underneath thee are the everlasting arms.'...

Depend upon it, the spirit of the Lord did n't pitch me into this seething caldron for nothing, and the Son of Man walketh with me in the fire."

The great reality above all other realities that filled the thoughts by day and the dreams by night of both Professor and Mrs. Stowe was that of the Eternal Goodness, —

"Oh Love divine that stooped to share,
Our sharpest pang, our bitt'rest tear."

The older they grew the more childlike and simple was their faith. At last came the time when Professor Stowe's increasing infirmities made the journey back and forth impossible, and Mrs. Stowe writes of the Mandarin home, that Southern paradise where she had passed so many happy years: "I am quietly settled down for the winter in my Hartford home.... It has become clear that Mr. Stowe cannot take the journey. We dare not undertake it. Our Southern home has no such conveniences as an invalid needs. It was charming while Mr. Stowe was well enough to sit on the veranda and take long daily walks, but now it is safer and better that we all stay with him here." CHAPTER IX DELINEATOR OF NEW ENGLAND LIFE AND CHARACTER

Mrs. Stowe began her literary career as a delineator of New England life and character. Her first success was " Uncle Lot"; a New England character sketch. She was an artist by nature and would have been impelled to literary expression under any circumstances, and the field in which she would most naturally have exercised her talents was in portraying the people and life of New England. By an accident of her life she was brought in contact with slavery and the Anti-Slavery movement. In this field she achieved her first and greatest triumph. Yet so acute a critic as Mr. Lowell said in reviewing "The Minister's Wooing": "It has always seemed to us that the AntiSlavery element in the two former novels of Mrs. Stowe stood in the way of the appreciation of her remarkable genius, at least in her own country.... Mrs. Stowe seems in her former novels to have sought a form of so-

ciety alien to her sympathies, and too remote for exact study, or for the acquirement of that local truth which is the slow result of unconscious observation. There can be no stronger proof of the greatness of her genius, of her possessing that conceptive faculty which belongs to the higher order of the imagination, than the avidity with which 'Uncle Tom' was read at the South. It settled the point that this book is true to human nature if not minutely so to plantation life.

"If capable of so great a triumph where access must so largely depend on the sympathetic insight of her mere creative power, have we not a right to expect something far more in keeping with the requirements of art, now that her wonderful eye is to be the mirror of familiar scenes, and in a society in which she was bred, and of which she has seen so many varieties, and that, too, in a country where it is most naive and original? It is a great satisfaction to us that in 'The Minister's Wooing' she has chosen her time and laid her scenes amid New England habits and traditions. There is no other writer who is so capable of perpetuating for us, in a work of art, a style of thought and manners which railroads and newspapers will soon render as palaeozoic as the mastodon, or the megalosaurians."

The summer of 1857 Mrs. Stowe was well-nigh crushed beneath the weight of a great sorrow, — the death of her eldest son. She dreaded everything that she did. As she afterwards said: " I sat hour after hour before my inkstand dreading to begin. I let my plants die by inches, and did not water them. I felt as if I were slowly freezing to death!"

Yet it was in this time of sorrow and heaviness that she began composing both "The Minister's Wooing" and "The Pearl of Orr's Island." Of the latter she says: "I seem to have so much to fill my time, and yet there is my Maine story waiting. However, I am composing it every day, only I greatly need living studies for filling in of my sketches. There is ' Old Jonas' my 'fish father,' sturdy, independent fisherman farmer, who in his youth sailed all over the

world and made up his mind about everything. In his old age he attends prayer-meetings and reads ' The Missionary Herald.' He has also plenty of money in an old brown sea-chest. He is a great heart with an inflexible will and iron muscles. I must go to Orr's Island and see him again."

Here we see the promptings of Mrs. Stowe's artistic nature. Had it not been for the "Key" and "Dred," we should have had this idyl of the coast of Maine in all the perfection of quiet beauty. Mrs. Stowe needed only the slow results of unconscious observation to have brought forth "The Pearl of Orr's Island," rich with local truth and color. As it was, this poor little flower of her genius was starved. She turned all her energies to the completion of "The Minister's Wooing," and "The Pearl of Orr's Island" was for the second time indefinitely postponed.

The reason for this is easy to understand. The Maine story was now too filled with sad memories of her lost son. She could not write upon it without Henry's face seeming to look upon her sadly from out the past happy days in Brunswick. When she visited Maine to prepare herself for the task she wrote to her daughters: " We have visited the old pond, and, if I mistake not, the relics of your old raft are there caught among the rushes. I do not realize that one of the busiest and happiest of the train that once played there shall play there no more.... I think I have felt the healing touch of Jesus of Nazareth on the deep wound in my heart, for I have golden hours of calm when I say, 'Even so, Father; for so it seemed good in thy sight.'" Yet the wound thus healed would ever and again break out and bleed af resh. There were memories in the Maine story that pierced her heart as with a knife. Like the flowers she planted over her son's grave that bloomed, and died, and bloomed again, so were the consolations that came to her soul. Under these circumstances " The Minister's Wooing " was nearer to her mood. Suffering, sympathy, sorrow, are its undertone. More than all the problems of the soul came the question, Where was her Henry now?" If ever I was conscious of an attack of the devil trying to separate me from the love of Christ, it was for some days after the terrible news came. I was in a great state of physical weakness, most agonizing, and unable to control my thoughts. Gloomy doubts as to Henry's spiritual state were rudely thrust upon my soul. It was as if a voice said to me: 'You trusted in God did you? You believed that He loved you? You had perfect confidence that He would never take your child till the work of grace was mature? Now He has hurried him into eternity without a moment's warning, without preparation, and where is he?'" It was inevitable that such reflections should come to the daughter of Lyman Beecher, to a New England Christian of the Evangelical faith. They have come to multi tudes; but there is no power that can so effectually shatter the stern logic of Calvinistic orthodoxy as the open grave. In "The Minister's Wooing" she met this problem, and thought and wrote herself out of her doubts and her agony. In Mrs. Marvyn's anguish when she receives the news of her son's sudden death at sea we have Mrs. Stowe's own heart laid bare. Then, too, there was the problem of suffering! That also she met in the doctrine of The Divine Sorrow regnant on the throne of the universe. So it is quite evident why "The Pearl of Orr's Island," though first taken up, was laid aside for "The Minister's Wooing." Two years afterwards, when she turned to it again, she wrote, as says Mrs. Fields in the " Life and Letters": "Authors are apt, I suppose, like parents, to have their unreasonable partialities. Everybody has,—and I have a pleasure in writing 'Agnes of Sorrento' that gilds this icy winter weather. I write my Maine story with a shiver, and come back to this as to a flowery home where I love to rest."

"The Minister's Wooing" was very largely dictated, and chapter after chapter thrown off at white-heat. Each chapter as finished she read before the assembled family in a particular corner of the long parlor of the old Stone Cabin at Andover. Her son Charles remembers vividly these family readings. The Professor with his long gray beard, white hair, and piercing black eyes, sat with his pocket handkerchief spread out upon his knees, alternately shaking with laughter, or heaving with sobs. Now and then with commanding voice he would point out an error or inadequacy in the argument on some point of theology, or call attention to a lack of local color in some descriptive passage. Such changes as he suggested Mrs. Stowe made immediately and without discussion. She never for a moment doubted the infallibility of her " rabbi" as she fondly called him.

Mrs. Stowe's oldest daughters, or the "girls," as they were always called, sat in judgment on the love-making, and in their department were as meekly obeyed as their father in his. The atmosphere of Mrs. Stowe's audience was, however, one of admiration. As Mrs. Fields says with truth in the "Life and Letters," in commenting upon Mrs. Stowe's craving for sympathy when she was writing: "It was a touching characteristic to see how the 'senate of girls,' or of such household friends as she could muster wherever she might be, were always called in to keep up her courage, and to give her a sympathetic stimulus. During the days when she was writing it was never safe to be far away, for she was rapid as light itself, and before a brief hour was ended we were sure to hear her voice calling, ' Do come and hear, and tell me how you like it!'"

Mrs. Stowe writes to one of her children at this time: "I have set many flowers around Henry's grave which are blossoming: pansies, white immortelle, white petunia, and verbenas. Papa walks there every day, often twice or three times.... To-night I sat there; the sky so beautiful, all rosy, with the silver moon looking out of it. Papa said with a deep sigh, 'I am submissive, but not reconciled.'" In both Professor and Mrs. Stowe there was no characteristic more strongly marked than their constant sense of the supernatural and the nearness of the world of spirits. Henry's grave was to them a charmed spot, for there he seemed nearer to them. Their son Charles well remembers their communings at this oft visited grave.

"Are they not all ministering spirits sent to minister unto them that shall be the heirs of salvation?" was the scriptural text most often on their lips. One day Mrs. Stowe climbed on a step ladder to fix the curtains in her room. She fell and marvelously escaped serious injury. The Professor heard her fall, and rushing into the room, found her prostrate on the floor. When he had assured himself that she was not seriously injured, he exclaimed with the utmost sincerity, " Oh, my dear, it was Henry's spirit that saved you!" She looked up into his face, and said, "He shall give his angels charge over thee, and they shall bear thee up in their hands."

It was impossible for Mrs. Stowe to treat " The Minister's Wooing" merely as a work of literary art. There lay behind it too many vital experiences which she could not make public, and which overbore the ordinary rules of literary composition. She wrote into it her heart anguish, as Tennyson wrote his into the lyrics that make up "In Memoriam."

The first conception of " The Minister's Wooing" came to her in Newport, Rhode Island, during the summer of 1830. Her brother William began his ministry there, and she went to visit him. She became acquainted with the facts of the life and ministry of the Rev. Samuel Hopkins. What first fixed her attention was the inherent unselfishness and nobleness of his character as illustrated by his conduct in fearlessly denouncing slavery before his slave-holding and slave-trading congregation. She was struck and thrilled by the thought that beneath the crust of dogmatic theology there could beat a heart so true to the noblest instincts of humanity. Instantly about this nucleus there gathered the memory of the heartbreak and anguish through which her sister Catherine had passed, and of which she herself had felt sympathetic vibrations.

There then floated before her mind the outline of a possible story in which these elements were to be combined. The thought of introducing love into the tale, as she afterwards did, came to her even then. To show the noble unselfishness of the Puritan divine he was to be in love with a member of his flock, a sweet Christian girl with a wild sailor lover. At the end the good minister shows himself capable of such supreme unselfishness in giving her up as to change completely the young man's attitude toward the Church and instituted Christianity by showing him that a creed is after all a plastic thing, and that even the stern hereditary faith of New England had in it elements of tenderness and beauty. It is interesting to note that though Mr. Whittier knew nothing of this original conception of "The Minister's Wooing," yet it was this motif that he emphasizes in his poem read at Mrs. Stowe's birthday party.

"Welcome of each and all to her
Whose wooing of the Minister
Revealed the warm heart of the man
Beneath the creed-hound Puritan,
And taught the kinship of the love,
Of man below and God above."

To this original conception of "The Minister's Wooing," born in the pain and anguish that came upon her through Henry Stowe's death, was added the cheerful pragmatism of old Candace: "So don't you go to laying on your poor heart what no mortal creeter can live under; 'cause as we's got to live in dis yer world, it's quite clar de Lord must ha' fixed it so we can; and ef things was as some folks suppose, why, we could n't live, and dar wouldn't be no sense in anything dat goes on.

"I 'm clear Mass'r James is one o' de 'lect; and I'm clear dar's considerable more o' de 'lect dan people tink. Why, Jesus didn't die for nothing, — dat love ain't gwine to be wasted. De 'lect is more 'n you or I knows, Honey!. .. and ef Mass'r James is call and took, depend upon it de Lord has got him...."

Here, also, is the echo of the soul struggles of her sister Catherine after the death of her lover, Professor Fisher.

After the first two or three chapters of "The Minister's Wooing" had been received, Mr. Lowell, then editor of the *Atlantic Monthly,* wrote to Mrs. Stowe a letter full of encouragement. Among other things he said: "When I got the first number of the MS., I said to Mr. Phillips that I thought that it would be the best thing you had done, and what followed has only confirmed my first judgment. q..

"You are one of the few persons lucky enough to be born with eyes in your head, — that is, with something behind the eyes that makes them of value....

"As for 'theology,' it is as much a part of daily life in New England as in Scotland, and all I should have to say about it is this, let it naturally crop out where it comes to the surface; but don't dig down to it. A moral aim is a fine thing, but in making a story an artist is a traitor who does not sacrifice everything to art...."

Mr. Ruskin with fine literary instinct felt that Mrs. Stowe, for reasons to him unknown, had not entirely followed Mr. Lowell's advice, for he wrote to her after reading the book: "Still I know well that in many respects it was impossible for you to treat this story merely as a work of literary art. There must have been many facts that you could not dwell upon, and which no one may judge by common rules."

If Mrs. Stowe in any way fell short of Mr. Lowell's ideal in "The Minister's Wooing" she certainly meant to redeem herself in "Oldtown Folks." She wrote to Mr. Fields in 1868, "My own book, instead of cooling, boils and bubbles daily and nightly, and I am pushing and spurring like fury to get to it."

"The story which had so taken possession of her mind and heart," remarks Mrs. Fields, " was ' Oldtown folks,' the one which she at the time fancied the best calculated of all her works to sustain the reputation of the author of 'Uncle Tom's Cabin.'"

The many proofs of her own interest in it seem to show that she had been moved to a livelier and deeper satisfaction in this creation than in any of her later productions. She writes respecting it, "It is more to me than a story; it is my resume' of the whole spirit and body of New England, a country which is now exerting such an influence on the civilized world that to know it truly becomes an object."

In her preface to the book she has said: "My object is to interpret to the world the New England life and character in that particular time in its history that may be called the seminal period. I would endeavor to show you New England in its seed-bed, before the hot suns of modern progress had developed its sprouting germs into the great trees of to-day.... New England people cannot be so interpreted without calling up many grave considerations and necessitating some serious thinking.

"In doing this work I have tried to make my mind as still and passive as a looking-glass, or a mountain lake, and then to give you the images reflected there. I desire that you should see the characteristic persons of those times, and hear them talk; and sometimes I have taken an author's liberty of explaining their characters to you, and telling you why they talked and lived as they did.

"My studies for this object have been PreRaphaelite, — and taken from real characters, real scenes, and real incidents. And some of the things that may appear most romantic and like fiction are simple renderings and applications of facts....

"In portraying the various characters that I have introduced, I have tried to maintain the part simply of a spectator. I propose neither to teach nor preach through them, any farther than any spectator of life is preached to by what he sees of the workings of human nature around him.

"Though Calvinist, Arminian, High-Church Episcopalian, sceptic, and simple believer all speak in their turn, I merely listen, and endeavor to understand and faithfully represent the inner life of each. I myself am but the observer and reporter, seeing much, doubting much, questioning much, and believing with all my heart only in a very few things."

Mrs. Stowe found it no easy task to carry out this conception. For three long years or more the story, or whatever it may most fittingly be called, dragged its weary length along. She wrote to Mr. Fields: "As my friend Sam Lawson says,' There's things that can be druv, and then again there's things that can't,' and this is that kind, as has to be humored. Instead of rushing on, I have often turned back and written over with care, that nothing that I wanted to say might be omitted; it has cost me a good deal of labor to elaborate this first part, namely, to build my theatre and to introduce my actors,..." The fact is the brave little woman was hard pressed by many cares, — an insufficient income, an invalid husband, and domestic griefs. She could certainly have done better work at this time had it not been for the grinding necessity she was under of writing for money.

"The thing has been an awful tax and labor," she writes again, "for I have tried to do it well. I may also say to you confidentially, that it has seemed as if every private care that could hinder me as woman and mother has been crowded into just this year that I have had this to do."

Again before she sails for Florida she writes to Mr. Fields: " A story comes, grows like a flower, sometimes will and sometimes won't, like a pretty woman. When the spirits will help I can write. When they a float, make faces, and otherwise maltreat me, I can only wait humbly at their gates, and watch at the posts of their doors."

The material for "Oldtown Folks" was furnished by Professor Stowe. "Oldtown" was the Natick of his boyhood, a little hamlet some twentyfive miles from Boston, now known as South Natick. Before beginning the story, Mr. and Mrs. Stowe made frequent and extended visits to the place. In the main the characters and the events were as he remembered and reported them to her. That they lost nothing in dramatic interest or quaintness by passing through the alembic of his mind is very certain. Professor Stowe was an inimitable story-teller, with an inexhaustible fund of humor. As a gentleman once remarked in view of a visit from him: "We must eat all we can before Professor Stowe comes, for after he arrives,

I doubt if we can eat anything, he will keep us laughing so!" Nearly every character and incident not only in "Oldtown Folks," but in the "Oldtown Fireside Stories," were familiar to the whole Stowe family, from their having heard of them repeatedly from Professor Stowe's lips, many years before they were committed to writing. Yet Mrs. Stowe was not writing history or biography, but, as she has said, "interpreting to the world New England life and character at a particular time of its history." Her aim was not to give an accurate portraiture of departed worthies of South Natick, which would have been at best a dreary and unprofitable enterprise. Some characters, however, are drawn to the life more nearly than others. Horace Holyoke is, for example, in spite of wide deviations from fact, Professor Stowe himself.

Professor Stowe's father was not an anaemic, consumptive schoolmaster, but a jolly, jovial baker, the life of the village. He died early, leaving a widow and two boys, William and Calvin. Calvin's mother was the daughter of Deacon William Bigelow, the Deacon Badger of "Oldtown Folks." The " Uncle Bill" of the book was Professor Stowe's uncle, William Bigelow, who graduated from Harvard College in 1793. He was a brilliant but eccentric character, and in his day a writer, and possessed inexhaustible fecundity as a maker of rhymes. For many years he was the Headmaster of the Boston Latin School, where he accompanied his instructions by the most Astonishing extempore rhymes, as, for example: —

"If **you** 'll be good I 'll thank you,
Bat if you won't I 'll spank you."

After ruling over his intractable school for many years with a rod of rattan, if not of iron, he was finally hurled from his throne by an uprising among his pupils, of which Ralph Waldo Emerson, himself a student in the institution at the time, has given a graphic account.

The Indians that figure in " Oldtown Folks" are all drawn to the life, and even the names are authentic. William Bigelow was a great fun-maker and caricaturist, and Calvin Stowe was one of

his apt pupils. Uncle Fly, Grandma Badger, and Sam Lawson, together with many other characters of the book, are given largely as they appeared in the eyes of these two incurable humorists. Some of the characters are of a more recent date, as, for example, Tina, who was Mrs. Stowe's youngest daughter.

The supernatural element that is introduced so prominently into the book owes its presence to Professor Stowe's unusual psychic experiences. In March, 1872, he wrote to George Eliot: —

"My interest in the subject of spiritualism arises from the fact of my own experience, more than sixty years ago, in my early childhood.

"I then never thought of questioning the objective reality of all I saw, and supposed that everybody else had the same experience. Of what this experience was, you may gain some idea from certain passages in 'Oldtown Folks.'"

In a letter written to Mrs. Stowe shortly afterwards, Mrs. Lewes says, "I was much impressed with the fact — which you have told me — that he Professor Stowe was the original of the 'visionary boy' in 'Oldtown Folks.'"

Soon after the publication of the book Mrs. Stowe received from George Eliot the following encouraging words: "I have received and read 'Oldtown Folks. ' I think that few of your readers can have felt more interest than I have felt in that picture of an older generation; for my interest in it has a double root, — one in my own love for our old-fashioned provincial life, which has its affinities with contemporary life, even all across the Atlantic, and of which I have gathered glimpses in different phases from my father and mother, with their relations; the other is my experimental acquaintance with some shades of Calvinistic orthodoxy. I think your way of presenting the religious convictions that are not your own, except by way of indirect fellowship, is a triumph of insight and true tolerance."

The very heart of "Oldtown Folks" as a delineator of New England life and character is the chapter called "My Grandmother's Blue Book." It is drawn from nature with what Mrs. Stowe has designated as "Pre-Raphaelite " exactness. It is a faithful portraiture of Mr. Stowe's grandmother, as he had known her, and through her of old New England: —

"My grandmother, as I have shown, was a character in her way full of contradictions and inconsistencies, brave, generous, energetic, largehearted, and impulsive. Theoretically she was the, disciple of the sharpest and severest Calvinism, and used to repeat Michael Wigglesworth's 'Day of Doom' to us in the chimney corner of an evening with a reverent acquiescence in all its hard sayings, while practically she was the most pitiful, easy-to-be-entreated mortal on earth, and was ever falling a prey to any lazy vagabond who chose to make an appeal to her abounding charity....

"She could not in cool, deliberate moments even inflict transient and necessary pain for the greater good of a child, and resolutely shut her eyes to the necessity of such infliction. But there lay at the bottom of all this apparent inconsistency a deep cause that made it consistent, and that cause was the theologic stratum in which her mind, and the mind of all New England, was embedded.

"Never, in the most intensely religious ages of the world, did the insoluble problems of the *whence,* the *why,* and the *whither* of mankind receive such earnest attention. New England was founded by a colony who turned their backs on the civilization of the Old World on purpose that they might have nothing else to think of. Their object was to form a community that should think of nothing else.

"Working on a hard soil, battling with a harsh, uncongenial climate, everywhere being treated by nature with the most rigorous severity, they asked no indulgence, they got none, and they gave none."

This conception of the inevitable connection between physical conditions and theological beliefs was a favorite one with Mrs. Stowe. Buckle could not have emphasized it more strongly. In 1873 she wrote from Mandarin, Florida,

to her brother Charles: "Never did we have so delicious a spring! I never knew such altogether perfect weather. It is enough to make a saint out of the toughest old Calvinist that ever set his face as a flint. How do you think New England Theology would have fared if our fathers had landed here instead of on Plymouth Rock?"

To turn again to her picture of the Puritan character in "Oldtown Folks ": "They never expected to find truth agreeable. Nothing in their experience of life had ever prepared them to think that it would be so. Their investigations were made with the courage of the man who hopes little, but determines to know the worst of his affairs.... The underlying foundation of life, therefore, in New England, was one of profound, unutterable, and therefore unuttered melancholy, which regarded human existence as a ghastly risk, and, in the case of the vast majority of human beings, an inconceivable misfortune."

We have only to recall what her own sister Catherine had written her brother Edward in 1822 to realize how this cheerless view of life had been early impressed upon Mrs. Stowe's mind: "I am most unhappy in the view which this doctrine presents of my own state and that of my fellow creatures, except the few who are redeemed from the curse. When I look at little Isabella, it seems a pity that she ever was born, and that it would be a mercy if she were taken away. I feel as Job did, that I could curse the day in which I was born. I wonder that Christians who realize the worth of an immortal soul should be willing to give life to immortal minds to be placed in such a dreadful world."

"There is something most affecting," to continue to quote from the book, " in the submissive devotion of these old Puritans to their God. Nothing shows more completely the indestructible nature of the filial tie that binds man to God... than the manner in which these men loved and worshipped and trusted God as the *All-lovely,* even in the face of monstrous assertions of theology ascribing to Him deeds which no father could imitate without being cast out of

human society and no governor without being handed down to all ages as a monster....

"I must beg my reader's pardon for all this, but it is a fact, that the true tragedy of New England life, its deep, unutterable pathos, its endurance and its sufferings, all depended upon and were woven into this constant wrestling of thought with infinite problems that could not be avoided, and which saddened the days of almost every one who grew up under it...."

To show how men and women were born, and lived, and loved, suffered, hoped, and feared, in this by-gone theological world, is the purpose of "Oldtown Folks." The otherwise unutterable gloom of the picture is alleviated by the quaint sayings and doings of Uncle Fly, Sam Lawson, and other mirth-provoking figures, that from time to time flit across the stage. The humor is the more effective because of the dark background against which it is shown. It ripples on the surface of the sadness of the life she is picturing as the sunlit waves dance on the bosom of the sullen stream, whose impenetrable depths no eye can fathom. In 1877 Mrs. Stowe wrote her last serial story. "Poganuc People" was to picture the scenes of her childhood as had " Oldtown Folks" those of Professor Stowe's. "Poganuc" was Litchfield, and "Dolly," Hattie Beecher. It is a complete autobiography of Mrs. Stowe's childhood. The old parsonage, with its garrets and cellars, yard and wood-pile, her father, her mother, and her brothers, Litchfield hills and walks, the orchard, the meadow, the mowing lot and the woods, the beautiful lakes and the clear-flowing Bantum River, are all sketched with loving fidelity. It is a pity that she had not done this earlier. As Dr. Holmes once said of her, "She was tired far into the future" long before she began it, and her days of authorship were all but spent. It lacks the strength and vigor of what she wrote of her reminiscences of childhood days for her father's "Autobiography and Correspondence"; but for all that it has a sweet and quiet beauty all its own, like that of a fading sunset sky.

When she began it she wrote to her son Charles: "I am again entangled in writing a serial, a thing I never meant to do again, but the, story, begun for a mere Christmas brochure, grew so under my hands that I thought I might as well fill it out and make a book of it. It is the last thing of the kind I ever expect to do. In it I condense my recollections of a by-gone era, in which I was brought up, the ways and manners of which are nearly as obsolete as the Old England of Dickens' stories.

"I am so hampered by the necessity of writing this story that I am obliged to give up company and visiting of all kinds and keep my strength for it. I hope I may be able to finish it, as I greatly desire to do so, but I begin to feel that I am not so strong as I used to be. Your mother is an old woman,... and it is best that she should give up writing before people are tired of reading her."

After it was finished she wrote to Dr. Holmes: "I sent 'Poganuc People' to you and Mrs. Holmes as being among the few who knew those old days. It is an extremely quiet story for these sensational times, when heaven and earth seem to be racked for a thrill; but as I get old I love to think of those quiet, simple times when there was not a poor person in the parish, and the changing glories of the year were the only spectacle."

In "Poganuc People" Mrs. Stowe figures as "Dolly."

"It was Dolly's lot to enter the family at a period when babies were no longer a novelty, when the house was full of the wants and clamors of older children, and the mother at her very wits' end with a confusion of jackets, and trousers, soap, candles, and groceries, and the endless harassments of making both ends meet that pertain to the lot of a poor country minister's wife." Here is a most faithful picture of the conditions under which she herself came into the world. And there follows a picture of her brothers as she remembered them in her childhood: "Dolly's brothers nearest her own age were studying in the academy, and spouting scraps of superior Latin at her to make her stare and wonder at their learning. They were tearing, noisy, tempestuous boys, good-natured enough and willing to pet her at intervals, but prompt to suggest 'that it was time for Dolly to go to bed,' when her questions or her gambols interfered with their evening pleasures."

The interest of the book turns largely on that event in the history of the State of Connecticut known as "The Downfall of the Standing Order," which took place through the adoption of a new constitution whereby the Congregational churches no longer enjoyed the peculiar privileges that had been theirs from the first; they were, in fact, disestablished. This was accomplished by a combination of many elements against the Federalists, among others the Democrats and the Episcopalians. Doctor Beecher was, of course, a staunch Federalist, and looked with consternation on what was transpiring about him and in spite of him. As he afterwards said to his children many times in looking back upon this period, "I suffered more than tongue can tell for the best thing that ever happened to the churches of Connecticut."

The day after the election he sat in an old rushbottomed chair in the kitchen, his face buried in his hands, and the tears trickling through his fingers, the picture of dejection and despair.

"What are you thinking about, father?" asked his daughter Catherine.

"The Church of God, my child! The Church of God 1" he sobbed. This scene made an enduring impression on Mrs. Stowe's mind in her childhood, and she has pictured it in " Poganuc People" as it took form in her memory.

"Dolly went to bed that night, her little soul surging and boiling with conjecture. All day long scraps of talk about the election had reached her ears. She heard her brother Will say that 'the Democrats were going to upset the whole state, for father said so.'

"Exactly what this meant Dolly could not conceive, but, coupled with her mother's sorrowful face and her father's agonizing prayers, it must mean something dreadful. Something of danger to them all might be at hand, and she said her 'pray God to bless my dear father and mother' with unusual fervor....

"In the morning, she sprang up, and dressed quickly, and ran to the window. Evidently the state had not been upset during the night, for the morning was bright, clear, and glorious as the heart could desire...."

Then, there is this real incident of her little girlhood. At family prayers her father poured out the anguish that oppressed his soul "in a voice tremulous and choking with emotion....

"Little Dolly cried from a strange, childish fear because of the trouble in her father's voice. The pleading tones affected her, she knew not why. The boys felt a martial determination to stand by their father, and a longing to fight for him. All felt as if something deep and dreadful must have happened, and after prayers Dolly climbed into her father's lap, and put both arms around his neck, and said, 'Papa, there shan't anything hurt you. I'll defend you!' She was somewhat abashed by the cheerful laugh that followed, but the doctor kissed her, and said, 'So you shall, dear! Be sure and not let anything catch me. ' And then he tossed her up in his arms gleefully, and she felt as if the trouble, whatever it was, could not be quite hopeless."

In the following extract we have the restful atmosphere of Mrs. Stowe's childhood: "It is difficult in this era of railroads and steam to give any idea of the depths of absolute stillness and repose that brooded in the summer skies over the wooded hills of 'Poganuc' Litchfield. No daily paper told the news of distant cities. Summer traveling was done in stages, and was long and wearisome, and therefore there was little of that. Everybody stayed at home and expected to stay there the year through. A journey from Litchfield to Boston or New York was more of an undertaking in those days than a journey to Europe is in ours. Now and then some of the great square houses on the street of Litchfield Centre received a summer visitor, and then everybody in town knew it, and knew all about it. The visitor's family, rank, position in life, probable amount of property, and genealogy to remote ancestors were freely discussed and settled, till all Litchfield was fully informed. The elect circle of Litchfield called on them, and made stately tea-parties in their honor, and these entertainments pleasantly rippled the placid surface of society. But life went on there with a sort of dreamy stillness. The different summer flowers came out in their successive ranks in the neatly kept garden; roses followed peonies and white lilies came and went, and crimson and white phloxes stood ranged in midsummer ranks, and the yellow tribes of marigolds brought up the autumnal season."

Goethe, in oft-quoted and familiar lines, has said that a talent is born in quietness and repose, but that a character is formed in the storm of life. Mrs. Stowe had both. She carried repose even into the storm of life, as if the quietness of those childhood days, pictured in "Poganuc People," had passed into her inmost soul. Just as she lived all phases, so she has portrayed all phases of New England; its restfulness and calm, its storm and stress.

One who had known and delineated New England life and character side by side with Mrs. Stowe, and who knew it as well and had portrayed it as truthfully as she, the poet Whittier, brings a fitting tribute to her in the lines: —

"To her whose vigorous pencil strokes
Sketched into life her Old town **folks,**
　Whose fireside stories grave or gay
In quaint Sam Lawson's vagrant way,
　With old New England's flavor rife,
waifs from her rude idyllic life."

CHAPTER X THE EBBING TIDE

One of Mrs. Stowe's most strongly marked characteristics was her love for and devotion to her friends. As she wrote to her friend Georgiana May, when still a very young girl: "The greater part that I see cannot move me deeply. They are present, and I enjoy them; they pass, and I forget them. But those that I love differently; those that I *love;* and oh, how much that word means!" There was nothing that she would not do for those she loved. Her

time, her strength, her purse, and everything that she had, was theirs. No gift was too costly, no sacrifice too great, to lay at their feet. This side of Mrs. Stowe's nature was to find its crowning manifestation in the publication by her, in the September *Atlantic* in 1869, of the article on Lord Byron which made her the storm centre of a perfect cyclone of adverse criticism.

She was at this time at the summit of her fame. Her name was a revered and honored one in thousands of homes and hearts on either side of the Atlantic. Whatever she wrote was read with confidence and appreciation. To jeopardize all this by dragging out into the light of day a scandal so reeking with moral rottenness as to befoul each and every mind that should come in contact with it seems, from a purely worldly point of view, recklessness little short of madness. She was urged not to do it; even her own husband plead with her and begged her to stay her hand. Her son Charles joined his father in urging her not to publish the article after she had read it to him at a quiet sea-side resort during the summer of 1869. But she set her face as a flint, and to every objection she said, in substance: "My friend Lady Byron is vilified, disgraced, and covered with infamy by the hand of Lord Byron's mistress! I know the truth in all this horrid business! I am one who can speak the truth that shall set her right before the world! If others who could speak would speak and clear her name of these vile slanders then I could be silent. I could never respect myself, nor have one moment's peace, did I keep silence at this time. I cannot, and I will not, sit calmly by and see my friend insulted, outraged, and her fair name trampled in the dust while I have it in my power to defend her!"

So she acted and braved the consequences, which were what her friends had foreseen. She felt most keenly the abuse that was hurled at her. Not all the denunciation that came upon her for the writing of " Uncle Tom's Cabin" was to be compared with that which this article brought on the devoted little woman. Deeply as she felt it, she was sustained

by the thought, "This is the sacrifice I bring to a dear friend who is silent in the grave, and for whom I speak as she cannot speak for herself." Constituted as she was, she could not have done otherwise. Where the reputation of a friend was to be defended, or the sacred trust which, as she felt, that friend had laid upon her was to be executed, there could be no counting of pain or loss. A colder and more cautious nature would have acted very differently under the circumstances. It gives the whole event a flavor of romance when we remember that Byron was the idol of her childhood. It was like a fairy story for her to be brought into such intimate relations with Lady Byron. It was like a tragedy for her to come out as the accuser of Lord Byron. Her son Charles vividly recalls his mother reading to him from "The Bride of Corinth" the scene where the spirit wife returning to earth gives her reckless and wicked husband time for repent ance while a cloud is sweeping over the surface of the moon, and her application of this dramatic message to the personal life of Lord Byron. She felt that Lord Byron was possessed by an insanity of wickedness that made him say, "Evil be thou my good!" Then she spoke of her conviction that there was great good in Byron, that he had a richly endowed and magnificent being. She evidently felt as her father had felt when he said, "Oh, I'm sorry that Byron 's dead. I did hope he would live to do something for Christ. What a harp he might have swept!"

Even more intense than Mrs. Stowe's devotion to her friends was her love for her children. There was an overflowing of her heart at times that made her whole being tremulous with love. She loved all her children with an equal bountifulness, but any weakness, sickness, or waywardness only intensified the love that loved the more, the more the need of love. So when her son, Captain Fred Stowe, came out of the war shattered in mind and body, it was upon him she poured out all the richness of her affection. Over his saddened spirit and wrecked and ruined life she hovered, throwing about him an atmosphere of tender protection. Since the all but fatal wound which he had received on the field of Gettysburg, the poor fellow was so infirm of purpose and weak of will that he was swept hither and thither by the impulse of the moment. Loving his mother most devotedly, and longing to be to her what he felt he ought to be, he lacked the will power to resist temptation. Everything was done that could be done. For his sake the Florida place was purchased. His father undertook a voyage to Spain in his company and for his benefit. The years that Mrs. Stowe was writing "Oldtown Folks" were years of crushing domestic grief, largely on account of this invalid son. At last, feeling that he was too heavy a burden to his mother, and that she had done all she could for him, he took passage on a ship, and sailed away around Cape Horn to San Francisco. This was all unknown to his mother, and came as a great shock. On the arrival of the ship in San Francisco, he was met by friends and taken to a hotel. He went out from the hotel, saying that he would return in a few minutes. Though every effort was made by the police, from that hour to this there has been nothing to throw the least light upon his fate. In spite of his infirmities, acquired in fighting for his country, he was one of the most lovable of men. He had many and unusual excellences of character, beside rare endowments that might have made him a blessing to his kind in his profession as a physician. His last act, even if misguided, was unselfish and noble. Having in vain tried and tried again to conquer his faults, he felt that he must go away and never return home unless and until he should again become master of himself. God only knows how constantly his mother watched and waited and longed for his return. She writes to a friend who has lost a son, "Think of your blessedness by my sorrow. Where is my poor Fred? You know where Frank is, and that he is safe and blessed. I never forget my boy. Can a woman forget her child?" She could not give him up; and at the last, when her mental powers began to fail, it was of him she

talked most constantly, and for him that her heart yearned with a longing unutterable.

In the autumn of 1871 Mrs. Stowe writes to her daughters: "I have at last finished all my part in the third book of mine that is to come out this year, to wit, 'Oldtown Fireside Stories,' and you can have no idea what a perfect luxury of rest it is to have no literary engagements, of all kinds, sorts, or descriptions. I feel like a poor woman I once read about, —

'Who always was tired,
Cause she lived in a house
Where help was n't hired,'
and of whom it is related that in her dying moments,—

'She folded her hands
With latest endeavor,
saying nothing, dear nothing,
Sweet nothing forever.'

I am in about her state of mind. I luxuriate in laziness. I do not want to do anything nor to go anywhere. I only want to sink down into the lazy enjoyment of living." It would seem that she had earned the right to "sink down into the lazy enjoyment of living" if any one ever had. She had at this time written twenty-three books in addition to short stories, essays, letters of travel, and magazine articles well-nigh innumerable. With all this already accomplished there were still in waiting seven books to be written before the close of her literary career.

In 1872 a new and remunerative field opened to her, which, though it entailed a formidable amount of hard and exhausting work, she entered upon with the ardor and enthusiasm of youth. It was a proposal from the American Literary Bureau of Boston to deliver a course of forty readings from her own works in the principal cities of New England. The offer was a liberal one, she needed the money, and so accepted it on condition that all should be over in time for her to return to her Florida home in December,— a month or so later than was her habit. She begins her lectures, and writes to her husband that she thinks it " on the whole as easy a way of making money as she has ever

tried, though no way of making money is perfectly easy." Professor Stowe, as usual, is heart-broken over her absence from home, and writes her a most dismal epistle, threatening to die if she does not come home immediately. To this letter she replies half-playfully, half-earnestly, "Now, my dear husband, please do wait, and try to remain with us a little longer, and let us have a little quiet evening together before either of us crosses the river."

She evidently enjoys her audiences and they enjoy her, and she reads Sam Lawson stories till all are dissolved in laughter. Manifestly her personality was the chief attraction. One woman, absolutely deaf, came up to her after one of her readings, and said, " Bless you. I come just to see you, and I 'd ruther see you than the Queen." Another woman introduced her two daughters, the oldest named Harriet Beecher, and the youngest, Eva. Nothing escapes her quick, observant eye as she travels. As she rides along the banks of the Kennebec she observes, " The scenery along this river is very fine. The oaks still keep their leaves, though the other trees are bare; but oaks and pines make a pleasant contrast." She finds a great difference in audiences. "Some audiences," she observes, " take the spring out of you and some put it in!" At last she writes: "Well, my course is almost done, and if I get through without any sickness, cold, or accident, how wonderful it will seem! I have never felt the near, kind presence of our Heavenly Father so much as in this, 'He giveth power to the faint, and to them that have no might He increaseth strength.' I have found this true all my life.... Well, dear old man, I think lots of you, and only want to end all this in our quiet home, where we can sing 'John Anderson my Jo' together."

The next winter she reads at the West, and visits her old home in Cincinnati. At Dayton she meets a woman whom she had known as a little girl in her brother George's parish many years before. Of her she writes: "Now she has one son who is a judge of the Supreme Court and another in business. Both she and they are not only Christians, but Christians of the primitive sort, whose religion is their all; who triumph and glory in tribulation, knowing that it worketh patience. She told me with a bright, sweet calm of her husband killed in battle the first year of the war, of her only daughter and two grandchildren dying in the faith, and of her own happy waiting on God's will, with bright hopes of a joyful reunion.... When I thought that all this came from the conversion of one giddy girl, when George seemed to be doing so little, I said, 'Who can measure the work of a faithful minister?'" After completing this Western tour Mrs. Stowe gave no more public readings, though she often read in private parlors for the benefit of churches and various charities.

After the death of Henry Stowe, the subject of spiritualism came to have an unusual fascination for his parents. Yet both of them came later into a more critical attitude with regard to the whole matter of physical manifestations. Professor Stowe came to a point where he doubted very seriously the objectivity of his own very marked and peculiar psychic experiences. It was about this time that Mrs. Stowe gave expression to the following views which may be regarded as her final conclusions on the subject after many years of meditation and patient research: "Each friend takes away a portion of ourselves. There was some part of our being related to him as to no other, and we had things to say to him that no other would understand or appreciate. A portion of our thoughts have become useless and burdensome, and again and again, with involuntary yearning, we turn to the stone at the door of the sepulchre. We lean against the cold, silent marble, but there is no answer, — no voice, neither any that regardeth. There are those who would have us think that in our day this doom is reversed; that there are those who have the power to restore to us the communion of our lost ones. How many a heart, wrung and tortured with the anguish of this fearful silence, has throbbed with strange vague hopes at the suggestion. When we hear some-

times of persons of the strongest and clearest minds becoming credulous votaries of certain spiritualist circles, let us not wonder: if we inquire we shall almost always find that the belief has followed some stroke of death; it is only an indication of the desperation of that heart-hunger which it in part appeases.

"Ah, were it true! Were it indeed so that the wall between the material and the spiritual is growing thin, and a new dispensation germinating in which communion with the departed blest shall be among the privileges of this mortal state. Ah, were it so that when we go forth weeping in the gray dawn, for the beloved dead, bearing spices and odors wherewith to embalm them, we should indeed find the stone rolled away and an angel sitting on it.

"But for us the stone must be rolled away by an unquestionable angel, whose countenance is as the lightning, who executes no doubtful juggle by pale moonlight nor starlight, but rolls back the stone in fair open morning and sits on it. Then, we could bless God for his mighty gift, and with love and awe and reverence take up that fellowship with another life and weave it reverently and trustingly into the web of our daily course. But no such angel have we seen, — no such sublime, unquestionable, glorious manifestation. And when we look at what is offered to us, ah, who that had friend in heaven could wish them to return in such wise as this? The very instinct of a sacred sorrow seems to forbid that our beautiful, our glorified ones should stoop lower than even to the medium of their cast-off bodies, to juggle, rap, and squeak, and perform mountebank tricks with tables and chairs; to recite over in weary sameness harmless truisms, which we were wise enough to say for ourselves; to trifle, and banter, and jest, or to lead us through endless moonshiny mazes. Sadly and soberly we say that if this be communion with the dead we had rather be without it. We want something a little in advance of our present life and not below it. We have read with some attention weary pages of spiritual communication purporting to come from Bacon,

Swedenborg, and others, and long accounts from divers spirits of things seen in the spirit-land, and we can conceive of no more appalling prospect than to have them true. If the future life is so weary, stale, flat, and unprofitable as we might infer from these readings, one would have reason to deplore an immortality from which no suicide could give an outlet. To be condemned to be bored by such eternal prosing would be worse than annihilation."

At the time that her brother, the Rev. Henry Ward Beecher, was passing through with that most painful experience of his life, — his trial in open court on certain charges involving his character as a man and a citizen, to say nothing of his standing as a Christian minister, — Mrs. Stowe wrote the following letter to her friend Mrs. Lewes (George Eliot): "I feel myself at last as one who has been playing and picnicking on the shores of life, and waked from a dream to find everybody almost has gone over to the beyond. And the rest are sorting their things and packing their trunks and waiting for the boat to come and take them. It seems now but a little time since my brother Henry and I were two young people together. He was my two years junior and nearest companion out of seven brothers and three sisters. I taught him drawing and heard his Latin lessons, for you know a girl becomes mature and womanly long before a boy. I saw him through college, and helped him through the difficult love affair that gave him his wife; and then he and my husband had a real enthusiastic German sort of love for one another, which ended in making me a wife. Ah! in those days we never dreamed that he or I, or any of us, were to be known in the world. All he then seemed was a boy full of fun, full of love, full of enthusiasm for protecting abused and righting wronged people, which made him in those early days write editorials, and wear arms, and have himself sworn in as a special policeman to protect poor negroes in Cincinnati, where we then lived, when there were mobs instigated by the slave-holders of Kentucky. Then he married and lived a missionary life in the new West, all with a joyousness, an enthusiasm, a chivalry which made life bright and vigorous to us both. Then in time he was called to Brooklyn, just as the crisis of the great Anti-Slavery battle came on, and the Fugitive Slave Law was passed. I was then in Maine, and I well remember his riding till midnight one snowy night to see me, and then our talking till near morning, what we could do to make headway against the horrid cruelties that were being practiced against the defenceless blacks. My husband was then away lecturing and my heart was burning itself out in indignation and anguish. Henry told me that he meant to fight the battle in New York, and that he would have a church that would stand by him in resisting the tyrannical dictation of slave-holders. I said, 'I, too, have begun to do something; I have begun a story trying to set forth the sufferings and the wrongs of the slaves.' 'That's right, Hattie!' he said,'finish it, and I will scatter it thicker than the leaves of Vallombrosa,' and so came 'Uncle Tom,' and Plymouth Church became a stronghold where the slave always found refuge and a strong helper. One morning my brother found sitting on his doorstep old Paul Edmunson, weeping; his two daughters, of sixteen and eighteen, had passed into the slave-warehouse of Bruin and Hill, and were to be sold. My brother took the man by the hand to a public meeting, told his story for him, and in an hour raised the two thousand dollars to redeem his children. Over and over again afterwards at Plymouth Church slaves were redeemed, Henry and Plymouth Church became words of hatred and fear through half the Union. From that time we talked together about the Fugitive Slave Law there has not been a pause or a stop in the battle till we had been through the war and slavery had been wiped out in blood. Through it all he has been pouring himself out, wrestling, burning, laboring everywhere, making stump speeches when elections turned on the slave question, and ever maintaining that the cause of Christ was the cause of the slave. And when it was all over, it was he and

Lloyd Garrison who were sent by the government to raise our national flag once more over Fort Sumter. You must see that a man does not so energize without making enemies.... Then he has been a progressive in theology. He has been a student of Huxley, and Spencer, and Darwin, — enough to alarm the old school, and yet remained so ardent a supernaturalist as to repel the more radical destructionists in religion. He and I are Christ worshippers, adoring Him as the image of the invisible God, and all that comes from believing this. Then he has been a reformer and an advocate of universal suffrage and woman's rights, yet not radical enough to please that reform party who stand where the Socialists of France do, and are for tearing up all creation generally. Lastly, he has had the misfortune of a popularity that is perfectly phenomenal. I cannot give you any idea of the love, worship, and idolatry with which he has been overwhelmed. He has something magnetic about him that makes men follow him, and worship him....

"My brother is hopelessly generous and confiding. His inability to believe evil is something incredible, and so has come all this suffering. You said you hoped I should be at rest when the first investigating committee cleared my brother almost by acclamation. Not so. The enemy have so committed themselves that either they or he must die, and there has followed two years of the most dreadful struggle. First, a legal trial of six, months, the expenses of which on his side were one hundred and eighteen thousand dollars, and in which he and his brave wife sat side by side in the court room and heard all that these plotters who had been weaving their webs for three years could bring. The foreman of the jury was offered a bribe of ten thousand dollars to decide against my brother. But with all their plotting the jury decided against them, and their case was lost.... This has drawn on my life, my heart's blood. He is myself; I know you are the kind of woman to understand me when I say that I felt a blow at him more than at myself. I, who know his purity, honor, delicacy, know that

he has been from childhood of an ideal purity, who reverenced his conscience as his king, whose glory was, redressing human wrong, who spake no slander, no, nor listened to it! Never have I known a nature of such strength and such almost childlike innocence. He is of a nature so sweet and perfect that, though I have seen him thunderously indignant at moments, I never saw him fretful or irritable,— a man who continuously and in every little act of life is thinking of others, a man that all the children on the street run after, and that every sorrowful, weak, or distressed person looks to as a natural helper. In all this long history there has been no circumstance in his relation to any woman that has not been worthy of himself, — pure,. delicate, and proper; and I know all sides of it, and certainly should not say this if there were a misgiving. Thank God, there is none, and I can read my New Testament, and feel that by all the Beatitudes my brother is blessed."

Almost ten years before this time Mrs. Stowe's strong, prophetic insight had led her to foresee that some such fate might one day overtake her best loved brother. In a letter to Mr. Howard of *The Christian Union,* she wrote: "I feel, the more I think of it, sure that the world that hates Christ is just as real in our times as it was in his.... I have pondered that question in relation to Henry's popularity; but I feel that the world really does *hate* him to a degree that makes it safe to hope that he is about right. Such demonstrations as now and then occur show that they are only waiting for him to be down to spring on him,... in proportion as he makes Christianity aggressive on sin they are malignant and will spring joyfully on him when their time comes."

It was about this time, 1882, that Mrs. Stowe wrote to her son Charles: "I have been looking over and arranging my papers with a view to sifting out those that are not worth keeping, and so filing and arranging those that are to be kept that my heirs and assigns may with less trouble know where and what they are. I cannot describe to you the peculiar feelings which this review occasions. Reading old letters, — when so many of the writers are gone from earth, seems to me like going into the world of spirits, — letters full of the warm, eager, busy life that is forever past. My own letters, too, full of bygone scenes of my early life and the childish days of my children. It is affecting to me to recall things that strongly moved me years ago, that filled my thoughts and made me anxious, when the occasion and the emotion have wholly vanished from my mind. But I thank God there is one thing running through all of them since I was thirteen years old, and that is the intense, unwavering sense of Christ's educating, guiding presence and care. It is all that remains now. The romance of my youth is faded, it looks to me now, from my years, so very young, — those days when my mind lived only in emotion, and when my letters never were dated, because they were only histories of the internal, but now that I am no more and never can be young in this world, now that the friends of those days are almost all in eternity, what remains?... I was passionate in my attachments in those far back years, and as I have looked over files of old letters they are all gone her oldest friends)... I have letters from them all, but they have been long in the spirit-land, and know far better how it is there than I can. It gives me a sort of dizzy feeling as to the shortness of life and the nearness of eternity when I see how many I have traveled with are gone within the veil. Then there are all my own letters written in the first two years of my marriage, when Mr. Stowe was in Europe and I was looking forward to motherhood, and preparing for it. Then my letters when my whole life was within the four walls of my misery, my thoughts absorbed by the developing character of children who have lived their earthly life and gone to the eternal one, — my two boys, each in his way good and lovely, whom Christ has taken in youth, and my little one, my first Char-, ley, whom he took away before he knew sin or sorrow, — then my brother George, and sister Catherine, the one the companion of my youth, and the other the mother who assumed

care of me after I had left home in my twelfth year, — and they are gone. Then my blessed father, for so many years for me so true an image of the

Heavenly Father, — in all my afflictions he was afflicted, in all my perplexities he was a sure and safe counselor, and he, too, is gone upwards to join the angelic mother whom I scarcely knew in this world, but who has been to me only a spiritual presence through life."

Nothing is sweeter than this devoted love that Mrs. Stowe and all her brothers and sisters bore to their mother. At the garden party tendered Mrs. Stowe on her seventieth birthday by her publishers at the home of ex-Governor ClaHin at Newtonville, Massachusetts, Henry Ward Beecher, when called upon to speak, had but one thought, and that was " Our Mother." He said: "Of course you all sympathize with me to-day; but, standing in this place, I do not see your face more clearly than I see those of my father and mother. Her I knew only as a mere babe child, he was my teacher and companion. A more guileless soul than he, a more honest one, more free from envy, from jealousy, and from selfishness, I never knew. Though he thought he was great by his theology, every one else knew he was great by his religion. My mother is to me what the Virgin Mary is to the devout Catholic. She was a woman of great nature, profound as a philosophical thinker, great in argument, with a kind of intellectual imagination, diffident, not talkative, such was the woman who gave birth to Mrs. Stowe, whose graces and excellences she probably more than any of her children — we number thirteen — has possessed. I suppose that in bodily resemblance, perhaps, she is not like my mother, but in mind she is most like her. "

From this time on Mrs. Stowe devoted herself to her husband, and refused to leave his side. She had very exalted ideals of what a wife should be to an invalid husband, and her devotion knew no bounds. He loved her with all the intensity of his being, and with his increasing weakness clung to her with the pathetic helplessness of a little child.

She went far beyond the limit of her physical strength in ministering to his needs, and probably in this way hastened the breaking down of her own constitution. For a long time she would not hear of having a nurse for him, and insisted on doing herself everything that his condition required, till at last compelled to yield him up to trained and skillful hands. If this was a failing, it may be truly said that " e'en her failings leaned to virtue's side." Professor Stowe died on the 6th of August, 1886. As the light of the setting sun shone into the room he opened his eyes, and apparently gazing far off beyond the distant hills, murmured to himself, "Peace with God! Peace with God," then closed his eyes and fell into a quiet slumber to wake no more. The death of her husband was followed in quick succession by the death of her brother Henry Ward, and her youngest daughter, Georgiana May. Georgiana was the most brilliant and gifted of all Mrs. Stowe's children, and was, in fact, the only one who could be truly said to have inherited real genius. Mrs. Stowe has drawn her to the life in the character of Tina in "Oldtown Folks"; Tina, whose self-will runs in the channel of the most charming persuasiveness. "She has all sorts of pretty phrases, and would talk a bird off a bush, or a trout out of a brook, by dint of sheer persistent eloquence; and she is always so delightfully certain that her way is the right one.... Then she has no end of those peculiar gifts of entertainment which are rather dangerous things for a young woman. She is a born mimic, she is a natural actress, and she has always a repartee or a smart saying quite apropos at the tip of her tongue."

Mrs. Stowe gives a letter of Tina's, every word of which might have been written by her own daughter, " Do you know, Aunty, I have got so that I can look exactly like a squirrel? We saw ever so many on the way, and I got a great many new hints on the subject, and now I can do squirrel in four or five different attitudes, and the boys almost kill themselves laughing." The loss of this child, after a long and depressing illness, was a crushing grief to Mrs.

Stowe. From this time on her thoughts turned away more and more from things of earth. "I have thought much lately of my leaving you all and going home," she writes to a distant friend. "I have come to that stage of my pilgrimage that is within sight of the River of Death, and I feel that now I must have all in readiness day and night for the messenger of the King. I have sometimes had in my sleep strange perceptions of a vivid spiritual life near to and with Christ, and multitudes of holy ones, and the joy of it is like no other joy, — it cannot be told in the language of this world. What I have then I know with absolute certainty, yet it is so unlike anything we conceive of in this world that it is difficult to put it into words. The inconceivable loveliness of Christ! It seems that about Him is a sphere where the enthusiasm of love is the calm habit of the soul, that without words, without the necessity of demonstrations of affection, heart beats to heart, soul answers to soul, we respond to the Infinite Love, and we feel his answer in us, and there is no need of words. All seemed to be coming and going on ministries of good, and passing each gave a thrill of joy to each, as Jesus, the directing soul, and centre of all, over all, and through all, was working his beautiful and merciful will to redeem and save. I was saying as I awoke:—

'T is joy enough, my all in all, At Thy dear feet to lie.
Thou wilt not let me lower fall,
    And none can higher fly.

This was but a glimpse; but it has left a strange sweetness in my mind."

It was about this time that she wrote to her brother Edward, "I feel about all things now as I do about the things that happen in a hotel after my trunk is packed to go home. I may be vexed or annoyed; but what of it? I am going home soon!" Shortly after this, in the last real letter which her sinking strength permitted, she writes to Mrs. Howard: "My sun has set. The time of work for me is over. I have written all my words and thought all my thoughts, and now I rest me in the flickering light of the dying embers, in a rest so profound that the voice of an old friend arouses me but momentarily, and I drop back again into repose...." The happy vision spoken of in this letter she was not immediately to realize. She was to become again a little child, free from all care and sorrow, wandering about the fields in summer, picking the flowers she loved so well, and singing the old hymns with childlike joy. "I love to sing this hymn," she would say, "for when I sing it I think I hear my mother's voice!" Little children were dear to her, and she smiled upon them, and greeted them as though she were one of them. She was as a little child, — a little child, gentle, loving, forgetful, and dreamy. She would rise early of a summer morning, when the dew was on the grass, and go out into the woods near her house gathering flowers. Then, on the impulse of the moment, she would trail her wet skirts through the dusty highway in utter unconsciousness of the result, and enter the house singing, "Then just before the shining shore," to be greeted with, "Oh, ma! Just look at your dress! Where have you been?" Her dress, she did not think of her dress; no, not as much as the birds of their feathers. Where had she been? She did not know, — she had not thought where she had been. Never fretful, never impatient, living only to love and to be loved, she moved about in a world all her own. A world of dreams where all was bright and hopeful, and where there were no burdens and no cares. She, who had suffered so much and so long, now suffered no more. If she suffered less, she loved more, till all her life was love. Waking at midnight, she said, "0 I have had such a beautiful dream!" Then as her faithful nurse gave her her medicine, she looked up into her face, and said, *I love you.* These were her last words on earth. She fell asleep to wake in heaven.

Lightning Source UK Ltd.
Milton Keynes UK
UKOW012006061112

201782UK00010B/35/P